When It's
Rush Hour
All Day Long

9/23/04

For Carol,
with grateful
appreciation —

Grace and Peace,
John Tadlock

Isa. 40:31
(KJV)

When It's Rush Hour All Day Long

FINDING PEACE
IN A HURRY-SICK WORLD

John W. Tadlock

new
hope
PUBLISHERS

Birmingham, Alabama

New Hope® Publishers
P. O. Box 12065
Birmingham, AL 35202-2065
www.newhopepubl.com

Library of Congress Cataloging-in-Publication Data
Tadlock, John W.
When it's rush hour all day long : finding peace in a hurry-sick world /
John W. Tadlock.
p. cm.
ISBN 1-56309-770-2 (pbk.)
1. Christian life. 2. Quality of life-Religious aspects-Christianity. 3. Stress-Religious aspects-Christianity. 4. Peace of mind-Religious aspects-Christianity. I. Title.
BV4501.3.T33 2003
248.4—dc21
2003008418

ISBN: 1-56309-770-2

N034121 • 1003 • 7.5M1

Dedication

To Lacey,
who for more than four decades
has tried to teach me that boundaries
actually enhance rather than restrict life.

Table of Contents

Foreword

Some books are meant to be read on the run. Others, like this one, are suited to be "front porch" books. *When It's Rush Hour All Day Long* is one of those reads that deserves and demands to be savored . . . and pondered . . . and meditated on . . . and laid aside for a spell now and then . . . and returned to over and over again for slow and steady consideration of words of comfort and ideas that afflict.

John Tadlock, "Tad" to those of us lucky enough to be his friends, has crafted a thoughtful book on a persistent problem. As you read, you'll get to know Tad, too, because he writes in the same voice and with the same openness he demonstrates in person. You'll quickly appreciate that there's a real, live, struggling, growing Christ-follower behind these pages. Tad doesn't play the expert. He admits that he has as many questions as answers. But he invites you along on his journey, his autobiographical pilgrimage toward deeper, sturdier faith. Most importantly, Tad has fully realized—earlier than most of us—that the light at the end of the tunnel is the headlight of an onrushing train! Ultimately, he has clearly decided to get on a new track with his life and spirit. We're invited to consider the same discipline.

As one who works with Tad every day, I can testify that one of the marks of over-stressed people—loss of humor—doesn't show up in him. Although often hurried, he hasn't lost his funny streak or his balanced outlook. His sense of perspective—the understanding that some aspects of life are just plain absurd and that God is the only one who doesn't mess up—is intact.

I can also tell you that the commitment to spiritual growth is evident day-by-day in Tad. As one of our young staffers said after Tad had led us in prayer, "When I die, I want Tad to pray me into heaven!"

So find a front porch, pull up a comfortable chair, and begin to read this book. You'll be challenged. You'll savor, ponder, listen to inner voices, pray, and grow. You'll laugh and brush a tear and probably redirect your life. Forewarned and forewarmed, risk the journey.

Bob Dale
Richmond, VA
August 2002

Preface

I don't recall ever having heard the term "hurry sick-ness" until John Chandler used it as a theme for a staff chapel devotional at the Virginia Baptist Resource Center. What I do remember was how deeply his remarks resonated with me. Therefore, I asked Chandler, the director of Virginia Baptist's Department of Evangelism and Church Growth, if he would share his notes with me. Working in collegiate ministry at the time, I was also serving an interim pastorate at the Antioch Baptist Church in "*The Goshen*" (local Virginia Baptist Association) in territory very familiar to such early Baptist luminaries as Lewis Craig, James Ireland, John Waller, and John Leland. After tweaking the sermon enough to satisfy myself that I had used at least two sources (enough to call it "research" rather than plagiarism), I preached the sermon for the folks at Antioch.

About a year later, I was asked to lead a conference for college students and campus ministers on the theme of "barriers to personal spiritual growth." Since I had come to believe that hurry is *the* most serious obstacle to an active, growing spirituality, I immediately suggested a seminar on "curing hurry sickness."

Sounded good to the planners, so I went to work on preparation for the seminar, adapting it for two different types of audiences: college students and their adult leaders.

Since that week in August 2001, I have found myself returning often to this theme in a variety of settings, including local congregations, adult leaders of college students, and of course, collegians themselves. It quickly became apparent that this subject is a live topic and one that many folks are interested in exploring.

Not long after that conference, I received a telephone call from Becky Yates, publisher for New Hope Publishers, asking if I would consider expanding the topic into a book. I was both surprised and flattered that a publisher might be interested in what I had to say on the subject. I gave the green light to a feasibility research project to determine what level of interest there might be. About 6 or 7 weeks later, I got the go ahead and Rebecca England, "my" editor, and I worked out the details.

Then I panicked. How do I write a book? One of the topics I deal with in the book is overload . . . and overload is often the result of not being able to say "no." And I had just said yes! Let's see, I do have a job that requires a good deal of time. I am serving an interim pastorate. I teach a course at the local Baptist seminary and occasionally am called on to lead winter Bible studies for local congregations in such studies as the Book of Revelation.

Additionally, I have a family: a wife who, although she has been very supportive—even screening my calls when I worked at home and allowing me to use her computer when the hard-drive on my laptop crashed (twice)—thinks it's a hoot that I am writing about how to "cure" hurry sickness. I also have two children, one of whom got married a few weeks prior to my deadline, two grandchildren, and aging and ailing parents who live 1,000 miles away. Overload? Busy-ness? Clearly, this book is autobiographical!

So I went to my colleague, Robert (Bob) Dale, whose office is just a few feet from mine—and who publishes a book about every two weeks—and I asked him: "How do you write a book?" His response: "Well, you take 100–150 pages and fill 'em with words!" (Thanks, Bob. Actually, he has given some invaluable tips and offered very helpful advice.) Dr. Reginald McDonough, retired executive director of the Baptist General Association of Virginia, also offered very helpful tips.

I owe deep gratitude to my collegiate ministries staff, who very often took up the slack when I was busy with writing, especially Terry Raines, my associate in the office. I want to thank several other staff who loaned books and offered suggestions: Susan Blanchard, Darrell Cook, and Pete Parks. Jason Thrower, a friend of many years and a Virginia pastor, graciously loaned me a few books. Others who suggested books and offered very helpful advice were Mike Clingenpeel,

Drexel Rayford, and Dan Bagby. My "state director" colleagues, Bill Choate (Tennessee) and Dean Finley (Missouri), offered useful suggestions.

I would be remiss if I didn't mention my wonderful assistant, Mary Neathawk, who, even in the midst of her own personal trials, helped me get through such annoyances as computer hard drive crashes and work-related deadlines. And during the summer of 2002, Abbie Duke, a student at Mary Washington College, did a great job of assisting in ways that went above and beyond the call of duty not precisely defined in her job description.

Thanks also to my new "boss," Dr. John Upton, Virginia Baptist's new executive director, who graciously consented to allow me a block of mostly uninterrupted time to complete the project, even in the midst of some very important "recasting" of Virginia Baptist mission and ministry. Rebecca England has been wonderfully understanding when I had to attend to matters related to family illness and when my computer "died" with only the first draft backed up. I thank her for that. Finally, thanks to all those who regularly asked, "What page are you on, Tadlock?"—which served as a regular prompt to keep at it even when I was much too busy.

I'm Just Wild About Hurry: The Hurry-Sick Quiz

"Anything worth doing is worth doing frantically!"
—Anonymous

I was in Shanghai, China, during the last week of June, 1997. The city, actually the entire country, was ablaze with excitement—Hong Kong was being returned to China after a century of rule by British government. Signs of exhilaration were everywhere but nowhere more clearly than in the Chinese people themselves. Everywhere we went, their warm hospitality was evident.

On the night of June 30, the eve of the turnover, our group witnessed a celebration that will probably go unrivaled in my lifetime. As we ventured from our hotel, we were inundated by Chinese who wanted to have their photographs taken with Americans. Some sidled up beside us and got friends to snap a picture, and others asked permission, especially of me. I finally figured out why: I'm about 6'2" tall, weigh more than I should, and wear a white beard. I look more like Colonel Sanders (whose image is easily recognizable all over China) than my traveling companions!

There were a number of celebrations going on, including the most incredible fireworks display I have ever seen. On the boardwalk of the Bund, a young man had at least a dozen plates spinning on the tips of stationary but flexible poles. I had seen this act on television, but never with that many plates. You've seen it. As soon as one plate started to wobble, he ran to give it another spin. The same happened with another, then another, and still another—one would be ready to topple off a pole and he would reach it just in time to keep it from crashing down to the concrete sidewalk.

That experience became a symbol for me of the way American culture has chosen to live. So many of us are like the young man spinning plates—we keep multiple plates spinning for work, family, church, even leisure. And it has just about done us in. This way of living has put so much stress on us that it has affected virtually all of our lives, especially the relationships that are most important to us. We can't escape it; nor can we ignore it.

Hurry has been identified as the greatest enemy of the spiritual life. Psychiatrist Carl Jung said, "Hurry is not *of* the devil; it *is* the devil."

Author John Ortberg tells a story in his book, *The Life You've Always Wanted*. He asked a friend for advice about how to live a spiritually healthy life, and after a long pause, the friend replied, "You must ruthlessly delete hurry from your life." Ortberg paused, thinking, "Okay, got it; now what else, 'cause I got things to do!" But his friend said, "There *is* nothing else."

The inference is clear: the dailiness of modern life is characterized by such frenzied activity and such a maddening pace that we are prevented from living as fully as possible into the contours of what it means to be a spiritually healthy, whole person.

Many of us fall prey to this disease even during the holiest seasons of the church year. For example, consider congregations that take seriously the importance of spiritual preparation for, say, Advent season. The rapid pace of life speeds up earlier and earlier each year as much of the world prepares for Christmas. Most pastors I know love the Advent season, partly because of the increased attendance at services. It is an important chance for churches to add a religious context to the season. But many also admit that they are happy to see it end because the pace of their lives has left them exhausted.

Hurry—Public Enemy Numero Uno

There is little doubt that hurry is, indeed, the enemy of one's spiritual life. Most of us who are a part of western culture live in a hurry-soaked world. Our lives are characterized by a frenetic pace, and this pace is symbolized in the business world. For example:

- *Citicorp* became the number one lender of money in this country when they cut in half the time it takes to receive the results for a loan application.

- *Denny's Restaurant* experienced huge growth when they stuck a timer on the table and promised a free dessert if the meal wasn't there within ten minutes.

- *Appleby's* and *Bennigan's* got in on the fun and upped the ante to a free meal.

- *Pert Plus* became the number one seller of shampoo when the company combined shampoo and conditioner in the same product; no more wasting time shampooing followed by conditioning.

- *Domino's* became the leading purveyor of pizza in America when they promised to get pizza to their customers in thirty minutes or less or the pizza is free. Their CEO is reported to have said, "We don't sell pizza; we sell delivery."

Technology: Blessing or Bane?

Modern technology is both blessing and curse when it comes to helping us save time so that we can have time for other things. Let's see . . . what are we talking about? We have fax machines, ATMs, voice mail, e-mail, instant messaging, drive-through, microwaves, pay-at-the-pump—all the results of technology designed to help us save time.

For much of my career I have worked in campus ministry, first as a campus minister at three colleges, then later working with other Baptist campus ministers in Virginia. During this time, the entering freshman students were more technology-savvy every year, and they had more devices to speed up the process of education. I typed my term papers on a typewriter, while these kids have laptops and printers. But the important issues they dealt with—making grades, making friends, making their own choices—stayed the same.

Even the comic strip character Sally Forth (written by Steve Alaniz & Francesco Marciuliano) is in this discussion. In one of the strips, Sally is talking to her pre-teen daughter, Hillary. In the strip, Sally opines: "People have always had a tendency to romanticize technology . . . . They thought the latest gadget would make their lives much easier. But thanks to cell phones, digital assistants, and laptops, now we can never *not* work. We don't have any excuses. We live in a work-obsessed society in which weekend getaways have replaced two-week vacations and FedEx even delivers on Sundays." Hillary: "So you're saying I can't have my own PalmPilot?" Sally: "I just don't want you to start down the wrong path."

Did she nail it or what? Her ideas are supported by some real medical heavyweights. Dr. Barton Sparagon, medical director of the Meyer Friedman Institute in San Francisco, studies stress-related illness and works with people to become aware of their stress and the impact it has on their lives. He believes the primary culprit for the increase in hurry sickness is our increasing use of technology. Powerful handheld computers and PDAs (PalmPilot and so on), pagers, and cell phones that have wireless Internet connections have made it possible to take our work everywhere with us—homes, cars, into our bedrooms, and on our vacations—literally anywhere.

The great invention of the 1980s was the overnight letter. Now, because documents may be sent via email attachment, the overnight letter is used only when you are *not* in a hurry. UCLA sociologist Jill Stein asserts that because the technology is available to us, there is an irresistible urge to use it.

I remember reading a TIME magazine article about a testimony that was given in 1967 concerning the future of time and labor. Apparently, a congressional blue-ribbon committee had conducted a study that showed technology would soon be developed to the point that the American working public would be able to save time so efficiently that people could choose to work either thirty weeks a year, twenty or thirty hours a week, or people would be retiring in their forties! The conclusion of this study was that the primary challenge Americans would be facing at the turn of the millennium would be what to do with all the excess time!

Well. How many people do you know whose principal challenge is deciding what to do with the extra time they have? Is that the primary challenge of *your* life?

Cultural Implications

Our commitment to these technological timesaving devices has clear results in our culture. I have asked this question to college students from all over the country: "If you had an extra hour to add to each day, twenty-five rather than twenty-four hours, what would you do with it? How would you spend it?" The number one answer? "I'd *sleep!*"

This is the sad reality. We live in a world where the most important task we have is to do as much as we possibly can as quickly as we possibly can. We are propelled forward with increasing velocity, and everything else is left in our wake. People are exhausted, stuck on fast-forward, and there is no pause button on our lives.

The Disease of Hurry Sickness

This is a condition which might be called "hurry sickness." Hurry sickness is not a new term by any means. In fact, the concept has been around since the 1950s. The term was coined by cardiologists Meyer Friedman and Ray Rosenman, who observed that heart disease patients had common behavioral characteristics, the most obvious of which was chronic rush.

How is hurry sickness defined? Perhaps the most common definition is the continuous struggle to accomplish more and more things, participate in more and more activities or events, in less and less time, often in the face of real or imagined opposition from others. In other words, hurry sickness is loading ourselves to the hilt with the "stuff" of life.

The Hurry-Sick Quiz

Take this quiz to help you know if you're hurry sick. Which of the following applies to you?

❏ You are driving and come to a traffic light. There is one car in each lane going your direction. Do you judge which will go faster, based on the make, model, and driver, so you can get behind that one? If so, you may have hurry sickness.

❑ If you judge wrongly and get behind the slower car, do you get really annoyed at the car in front of you? If so, you might have hurry sickness. (Someone has invented the "honkasecond"—the time between when a light changes and the car behind you honks!)

❑ You're choosing a check-out lane at Wal-Mart. Do you count the people in each line, estimate how much stuff is in their carts, and gauge the speed of the clerk? If so, you might have hurry sickness.

❑ Your hurry sickness is worse, however, if you choose line A but keep tabs of where you would have been in line B. If the person in line B checks out before you, you get angry and depressed. But if you get through first, it's like, "YES!!! I've won the Boston Marathon!"

❑ Do you find yourself getting impatient because a "time-saving" technology, such as an Internet connection, fax machine, printer, or email, makes you wait a few seconds? You might have hurry sickness.

❑ When you buy food, do you choose a large percentage of microwavable or "instant" food to reduce your cooking time? Do you cook a meal fewer than two times a week?

❑ Do you find yourself often doing two things at once—talking on the phone and typing, reading and watching television, driving and eating? Do you have magazines or books in your bathroom? You might have hurry sickness.

❑ Does driving to work become a contest to see how many vehicles you can pass? You might have hurry sickness.

❑ Do you speed on the highway, buying the theory that state troopers will only stop you if you exceed the limit by five miles per hour? (Take it from me, it just isn't true!)

❑ Do you have your quiet time with God while doing something else, such as exercising, walking the dog, or driving?

❑ Do you find yourself rearranging the clutter in your schedule, trying to fit more activities in while enjoying them less and less? You may have hurry sickness.

Hurry Up!

What are the symptoms of hurry sickness? How do you know if you have it? There are clear symptoms. If you have the symptoms, you probably have the disease. I have borrowed John Ortberg's list of hurry sickness symptoms.

First, hurried people constantly speed up the pace of their daily activities. There are just not enough hours in the day. There exists a constant sense of not having enough time to accomplish the items on your "to-do" list for today. One of the ironies is that the people with whom you interact don't seem to notice how much you have to do. A colleague of mine used to come into my office looking for a cup of coffee and some conversation. He would often say to me, "I don't have a thing to do and I'd like to do it *right here*!" I loved the line and have used it myself, but I *did* have things to do and it made me nuts that he didn't seem to understand that. I suspect that most of us have had to deal with people who just couldn't seem to comprehend the busy-ness of our schedules and were forever getting in the way, preventing us from accomplishing what needed to get done.

Polyphasic Activity

The second symptom of hurry sickness is polyphasic activity. Polyphasic activity is also known as multitasking; it means trying to do more than one thing at the same time. The person in a hurry is not satisfied with what she is accomplishing at a normal pace.

There are attempts to gain more time and accomplish more things by trying to do two or more tasks simultaneously.

During the summer of 2001, our local daily ran a story about a study that became the basis for New York state government to pass a law banning driving while talking on cell phones. The study was published in the August 1, 2001, issue of the journal *NeuroImage* and was led by Dr. Marcel Just. The report asserted that the conventional wisdom that the brain actually speeds up to compensate for multiple activities was not true. In fact, the study revealed that the brain appears to have a finite amount of space for tasks requiring concentrated attention. The researchers concluded that when people attempt multitasking activities, brain activity does not double; rather, it decreases. People performing two demanding tasks simultaneously do neither one as well as they do each separately.

Some suggest that the most common polyphasic activity of the hurried person is the habit of doubling up on conversations. Imagine this. You are at a social gathering when you encounter a friend. The friend gauges success in life by the number of people he can schmooze during an event. He is working the room, talking with as many people as possible when he stops to chat with you. You feel honored that you have been graced by the presence of the Great One. About thirty seconds into the conversation, your friend is distracted by someone else who walks by as you chat, and you realize that you don't have his undivided attention . . . and probably never did. Thinking about or doing something else while theoretically "listening" to another person is evidence of polyphasic activity.

It's common to become polyphasic in our spirituality. I have a colleague who often asks people when they pray. Would you care to guess what the most common answer is? "While driving!" The second most common answer is, "while showering." The point is, prayer for many people is not important enough as a single activity. Can't waste time just *praying*! We need to pray while doing something else.

Almost every day while driving to work, I see people doing a multiplicity of other things. I have seen men shave and women put on makeup at stoplights (and sometimes, while attempting to drive). I have seen people using cell phones and even *reading newspapers* while driving over the speed limit on interstate highways!

Our son was convinced that he could not study effectively unless he was watching television, listening to the radio, and taking an occasional phone call. We read, eat a meal, and watch television, all at the same time. Someone suggested that the ultimate indictment for hurry sickness is if your bathroom has magazines or books—so you can double up on *that* time. (Guilty as charged, your honor!)

Clutter

Another symptom of hurry sickness is clutter. Our lives are cluttered with too many things. There is too much to do, too many dates on the calendar. Life lacks simplicity. Take a look at your desk. Is it possible that the mound of papers and stuff reproduces itself? It seems that way to me, despite occasional times when my "cleaning gene" kicks in. I've tried to follow the advice of the late Ralph Winders, my first campus ministry boss in Mississippi. One of the lessons he tried to teach his minions was the importance of keeping one's workspace clean and orderly, and that the key to that was to begin working from the "top to the bottom."

Our Quaker friends have the concept of *cumber*—material and spiritual clutter that overwhelms our lives and prevents us from hearing God's voice. My daughter gave me a tape of a spirituality workshop she attended at Montreat Conference Center at Black Mountain, North Carolina. One of the speakers, Dorothy Bass, talked about this phenomenon, calling attention to the dazzling array of products available to the American public. She observed that we no longer go to the market. Now the market comes to us wherever we are. Go to any mall these days and you will see young people wearing advertising on their clothing. What a concept! Convince people that this is the coolest, most *chic* thing to do, and they pay good money to buy the opportunity to be a walking advertisement for

Tommy, Ralph, or any number of other business tycoons!

This is *cumber*, and it affects our lives in many ways. The stuff we acquire requires our energy and effort to get and to keep—only to toss when it either goes out of style or in the unlikely event that it is kept long enough to wear out! The problem comes when we fill our lives with it, and spend most of our time, energy, and creativity on accumulating, maintaining, and disposing of all this stuff. We eventually discover, to our dismay, that this cumber now *encumbers* us. And there is little time left for what is really important.

The Costs of Hurry Sickness

Accelerating the pace of daily activities. Polyphasic activity. Clutter. All symptoms of hurry sickness. What does it do to you? How does it affect your life? Here is a short list of the costs of hurry sickness.

One cost of haste is shallowness. We become shallow and superficial people. Ever hear the saying, "a mile wide and an inch deep?" Ever feel that way? We are living in wonderful times. It is, indeed, an information age. But I wonder if we have traded wisdom for information. It happens, I think, when we live in a hurry.

Microwaves have to be among the most outstanding inventions of the past fifty years. I don't know what we would do without ours. I am not suggesting that we return to the "good old days" and give up our timesaving devices. Microwaves are nice precisely because they *do* cut time. But substance and depth cannot be microwaved. Maturity cannot be microwaved. The sad truth is that many fall into a pattern of expecting to microwave just about everything.

Another cost of haste is the erosion or destruction of intimacy with God. When lack of time is a problem, prayer and meditation get pushed to the periphery of our lives. They are twin components in our development of a deep relationship with God. It's impossible to develop a substantive relationship with God (or anyone else) when you are in a hurry. As the great Diana Ross once taught us, "You can't hurry love. You just have to wait!"

Perhaps the highest cost of hurry is the erosion of our capacity to love. This is, of course, the other side of the intimacy-with-God coin. We cannot love God or people if we are constantly in a hurry. Hurry and love are fundamentally incompatible.

I'm thinking that the front-line casualty of hurry sickness is a damaged family life. My colleague John Chandler tells a story about bathing one of his young sons one night. Typically, the boy really enjoyed playing games, prolonging the time for bathing, for drying off, getting into his pajamas, and into bed. On this night John said to his son, "Hurry up, get out of the tub, and get toweled down!" His son finally got out, but started dancing around. John said, "Don't do that, we need to hurry!" His son stopped just for a moment and looked at him and said, "Why?"

No answer. No reason to be in a hurry. It wasn't quite his normal bedtime. Nothing was on the schedule for the rest of the evening. No agenda at all. Then John confessed, "Here's the truth. I'd just gotten into such a busy rhythm, rushing, bustling, scurrying about, that by that time I had become *addicted* to hurry."

Retreat

When I started this writing project, I felt the need to make some changes in my own life . . . to slow down, to become more intentional about giving my life some margins in order to function more effectively, if not more efficiently. One of the decisions I made was to take one day every month for a personal retreat, to take a full day and go somewhere out of the ordinary to pray, meditate, and just be quiet.

My first attempt to do this came at the end of a week following a major meeting for which I had ultimate responsibility. I talked with Pete Parks, campus minister at the College of William and Mary, and told him that I wanted to spend a day at Colonial Williamsburg, one of our favorite places in Virginia. My wife and I

especially love it in the fall when the leaves turn bril-
liant colors on the maple trees on Duke of Gloucester
Street.

Pete told me about some little-known walking
trails, and I set out on Friday morning for Williamsburg. I took a book my daughter had recommended
after participating in a silent retreat one weekend at
the Gethsemani Monastery in Trappist, Kentucky. My
intention was to spend some significant time in silence
and prayer and to do some reading that would deepen
my spiritual intimacy with God.

I put the book into my backpack and went to Mer-
chant's Square to get a cup of decaf and to enjoy
watching people, stopping to read a little of the book. It
went well for about thirty minutes. Then I started to
think about work-related things I needed to get done.

Mary, my wonderful, resolute assistant, would be getting a little anxious that I had not turned in my monthly
travel report, and it *was* on my things-to-do list. I had
everything I needed to do the report in my backpack, I
reasoned. "Well, it won't take long, and doing it now
means that I won't have it to do over the weekend." A full
two hours later, it occurred to me that I was working! I
was not spending the time as I had planned, in retreat,
recovering Sabbath—I was doing what I would be doing
if I had stayed in the office for the day!

That's when it dawned on me. My background and
experience had left such a strong impression in my
life that I had become convinced that anything not

related in some fashion to work is really a waste of time. Specialists say that it is possible to live in such a constant state of adrenaline arousal as to actually become addicted to hurry. And I am a living, breathing testimony to that assertion.

The Cure?

The costs of hurry are too high. I wonder how many there are like me who get to the end of the day and don't have energy to give to the people we love. What might we be able to do about this? What is the cure for hurry? Well, I don't believe it is laziness. It isn't becoming a slug. It isn't just to "veg out!" The opposite of hurry is not sloth. God wants us to slow down, to rest, and to experience Sabbath.

Sabbath is more than just spending the day resting. Sabbath is creating a space for God in your life, creating room for divine activity. Sabbath is giving up one day of self-directed goals and striving in order to make room for God to direct us. The practice of setting apart one day out of seven, while very practical and real, is also a sign for our need to make room for God in our everyday life, so that eventually it may all become God-directed.

The Bible has some very practical suggestions to offer. For instance, one of them is to get enough sleep! Sleep is an act of relinquishment and trust that God sustains us. It is the confidence that God will take care of my world, my job, my church, my children and grandchildren—and that one of the most important things I might do is to place my trust in God.

These are pretty hard words for some of us to hear. It sounds a bit odd, doesn't it, to suggest that perhaps the most spiritual first step you could take in your life would be to get a really good night's sleep tonight? The reason is that it is really hard to be Christian when you are tired. It is hard to be loving and joyful and patient when you are exhausted.

Author Brent McDougal confesses that "keeping the Sabbath" is one of the most difficult practices for him. I concur. It is very hard to practice Sabbath, to cease work and any other activity that spends your spiritual, physical, emotional, and psychic energy on anything that hinders you from becoming the person you were created to be. McDougal says in his book, *The River of the Soul: A Spirituality Guide for Christian Youth*, that "Sabbath keeping is perhaps one of the most accurate measures of how close I am to Christ."

How often do you hear people say (or say it yourself), "I just don't have enough time!" There is so much pressure to earn a living, nurture relationships, care for children or aging parents, stay physically fit, do the household chores, *ad infinitum*. The one clear, non-negotiable for all who are truly interested in forging a stronger relationship with God is taking the time, not just to nod God-ward, but to find a way to become intentionally focused toward God.

Wendell Berry sets the house in order with this poem:

> Whatever is foreseen in joy
> Must be lived out from day to day.
> Vision held open in the dark
> By our ten thousand days of work.
> Harvest will fill the barn; for that
> The hands must ache, the face must sweat.
>
> And yet no leaf or grain is filled
> By work of ours; the field is tilled
> And left to grace. That we may reap,
> Great work is done while we're asleep.
>
> When we work well, a Sabbath mood
> Rests on our day, and finds it good.

—From *A Timbered Choir,* by Wendell Berry.
© 1998. Used by permission.

CHAPTER TWO

The Costs of Hurry Sickness

"I have held many things in my hands and
I have lost them all; but whatever I have placed
in God's hands, that I still possess."
—Martin Luther

There are definite costs for hurry sickness. In the previous chapter we dealt briefly with some of them. Borrowing from John Ortberg, we said that there were several obvious costs to this insidious problem.

• There is *superficiality* or *shallowness*, the inclination to live life like a class we're auditing rather than taking for course credit.

- There is the *slow destruction of our intimacy with God*, having neither time nor energy to focus on the most important relationship we will ever have.

- There is *clutter*, the feeling of being inundated with people, places, things, noise, disorganization—which results ultimately in disorientation.

- Another cost is the *erosion of our capacity to love* those whom God has given to us by circumstance or by providence. Love takes time, the one commodity in short supply for those who are addicted to hurry.

John Ortberg wrote about something he called "sunset fatigue," a term he said was coined by Lewis Grant. He observes that those whom we love the most and to whom we are most committed often end up getting the leftovers, the residue from a busy, stress-filled day. And he lists several behaviors that are dead giveaways that one is one afflicted by hurry sickness:

- You continue to rush around at home for no reason.

- You have sharp exchanges with spouse and children, even when they are innocent of any reason for them.

- You find yourself hurrying your children along, sometimes even setting up mock races ("Okay kids, let's see who can take a bath fastest").

- You tell your family that everything will be back to normal in a week or two.

- You indulge in self-destructive escapes: too much television, abusing alcohol, surfing the web in order to explore sexual web sites.

- You flop into bed with no sense of gratitude and wonder for the day—you only feel fatigue.

Now I would like to turn more intentionally and in greater detail to these and other costs of hurry sickness.

Fatigue

Fatigue may be one of the most obvious costs of hurry sickness. In its less severe manifestations, fatigue can be a good thing. For example, it can be a warning sign that a change in your life is needed. We all know people who seem stuck on fast-forward, going 24/7. They may work flat-out for weeks at a time until they finally hit the wall and crash. Is that wise? Is it good stewardship of "God's temple"? Paying attention to the feelings of fatigue can help you avoid hitting the wall.

However, if fatigue is an ongoing way of life for you, you might not recognize the signs—fatigue becomes "normal" for you. Archibald Hart wrote about this in

Leadership Journal [1], saying that if your fatigue is severe and longstanding, it can be an indicator of more serious problems, such as biological depression, or a weakening of the immune system due to stress.

Have you been to an "action" movie lately? (My wife loves them.) If so, you have probably noticed how they assault your senses with breakneck images at an unrelenting pace. We saw one such film recently that was one tense, incredibly fast-paced scene after another. I remember saying to my wife about halfway through the film that I was *exhausted*. But this genre of film is pretty much a reflection of our culture.

One film critic observed that the best of these kinds of movies seem to insert periodic "breaks" from heavy-duty intensity, often using humor even in the midst of tragedy to create "down time." Ron Howard (Little Opie Taylor turned Oscar-winning film director) claims that this is no accident, that even action-packed movies look for ways to balance the harsh action with a semblance of calm so that moviegoers will leave the theater a bit more relaxed. Even Hollywood recognizes the importance of *balance* in life.

Fatigue can be either psychological or physiological. The kind of fatigue I am talking about, however, is a direct result of an accelerated pace of life. It is more than just being tired. It means that the cells of your body have become so depleted that you have lost vitality and the capacity to respond.

Jesus was certainly no stranger to this experience.

One story about how Jesus handled fatigue is the account in John 4 of when Jesus and His disciples came to a village in Samaria and sat down at a well. The Scripture says that Jesus was tired from His journey (John 4:6). So Jesus sat alone at the well as His disciples were getting food for them to eat. Commentators point out that Jesus sat at the well during the least likely time of day for others to come to it—high noon. (That is also significant regarding the story of Jesus' encounter with the Samaritan woman.) But a point that is often missed in this story is that when Jesus was fatigued, He sought solitude away from the chatter of people and the noise of busyness. And we see Him doing this throughout the pages of the Gospels.

That's why hurry has become the problem it is. It depletes our vitality and drains our energy. When we are fatigued in that way, it most certainly interferes with the important relationships in our lives and impedes our ability to function at our best in school, at work, with church, and even at play. In order for us to function effectively, it is important to understand and affirm the rhythms of work and rest.

Loss of Perspective

The loss of perspective is another cost of hurry sickness. Perspective means a balanced way of seeing things—the capacity to see people or things in their relationship to each other. You see things as they are rather than in some distorted manner.

It's hard to keep perspective when you're constantly hurried. Hurried people tend to experience a Cliffs Notes condensed version of life. In this country we have come to expect that the evening news shows will be able to tell us everything that is going on in the whole world in less than 30 minutes. In fact, the "teasers" at the top of each news broadcast take about five seconds each and are designed to create sufficient interest that viewers will stay tuned for a story that will take about three minutes to tell. There are entire offices stuffed with herds of professional staff in all the major television news outlets devoted to nothing but coming up with just the right teasers. One network executive admitted that almost as much time is devoted to this task as to the actual news broadcast itself. It's hard to develop a thoughtful perspective with little more than a "sound bite" coming in.

The college debate team probably taught me best to avoid characterizing everything too rigidly. The leaders of the national forensics organization, presumably, decided in those days what the national "question" was to be. Debate teams had to research both sides of the question and be prepared to debate either the affirmative or the negative.

When there was a debate tournament, no team knew in advance which side they would argue until a few minutes before the debate started. It was expected that both sides would be well-researched and the basic argumentative points chosen. It was then up to the debaters to build their respective cases and to rebut the opposing team in theirs. Clearly, the most effective debaters were those who could keep the kind of perspective that would enable them to argue both sides of the same issue convincingly.

Seminary professor William Hendricks used to warn students and others about "getting their exercise by jumping to conclusions." This is easy to do when you lack the time or the energy to ferret out alternative perspectives on a particular issue. Fatigue contributes to our tendency to define something totally on the basis of our limited experience—it makes us more likely to be insensitive, oblivious, and judgmental toward others. The inability to affirm both sides of an issue, or multiple perspectives, is often the result of fatigue. We are simply not able to allow the unique things of life to filter through our experiences.

In addition, our level of "ego investment" contributes to the loss of perspective. Organizational gurus have been nearly unanimous in their observation that colossal egos are the greatest detriment to needed change. Jim Collins, in his well-researched book *From Good to Great*, says that the most effective CEOs in the U.S., the ones who have led their companies to unprecedented growth and have been able to sustain that growth for an extended period of time, are called

"Level Five" leaders. One of the most important characteristics of that kind of leader is the lack of a huge
ego. These leaders are working for goals other than
personal aggrandizement or ego gratification. They
have gotten themselves out of their own way.

Dr. Wayne Oates writes in his book *Nurturing
Silence in a Noisy Heart* that "the most telltale evidence
of the loss of perspective is when you begin to belabor
the point in discussion, 'sweat the small stuff' in deci-
sion-making, procrastinate about big decisions, or
become inappropriately irritable with your fellow
workers, your family, or your friends. You are making
too many mistakes."

Loss of Equilibrium

Another cost of hurry sickness is the loss of equilibrium in our lives. Psychiatrist Dr. Louis McBurney discussed the bio-psycho-social impact related to
establishing boundaries in one's life in the "Pastor to
Pastor" audiotape series. [2] Although the focal point of
the tape was toward pastors, it's not much of a leap to
say that this is true for any person.

Louis McBurney says that we have to consider
the biological issues (nutrition and exercise), psychological factors (the psyche), as well as the social envi-
ronment when talking about the basic components
of a balanced life. He suggested that doing so was

absolutely necessary in order to achieve any semblance of a balanced life. When we fail to establish bound aries, it is highly likely that self-esteem might be the culprit. It is obvious, isn't it, that certain segments of our society have connected their sense of self-worth very closely with what they do? Perhaps one of the greatest stimulants for many people is the need to be needed.

This is certainly not a new thought. The idea that we need somehow to earn our way—a kind of "works right-eousness" approach to our existence—is at the center of many of society's problems and many personal ones, as well. I have struggled for years with my own need to be liked by everyone—which is probably number one on the list of the top ten unrealistic expectations. Nonetheless, this concept has been very influential in the way I have lived my life.

For example, my need to be liked has caused me to go out of my way to avoid conflict with almost everyone. I was the guy who refused to say anything to the server about how bad the food and service were in the restaurant. The notion that total harmony was the real queen of virtues was ground into my consciousness somewhere along the way, and for years I wanted to make sure that there was little possibility of potential discord.

In fact, when the waiter came to ask the obligatory "How is everything?" I would actually lie to him so that he wouldn't feel bad, and then I would leave a generous tip. (Of course our son Kelly, who worked as a waiter/busboy in several restaurants during college, taught me that leaving a tip says more about me than about the quality of the meal or the service and that I should drop a minimum of 20 percent every time.)

Our lives get out of balance when we have problems setting boundaries. Have a hard time saying "no?" Even when saying "yes" would make your life go off-kilter like an unbalanced washing machine cycle?

Picture this. It's Saturday morning, cleaning day— and part of the cleaning is doing the laundry. You put a huge load of dirty laundry in the washer and, although your spouse has counseled you time and again about how to actually load the washing machine, you persistently get it wrong. You go off to do some other chores, and suddenly you hear the most awful buzzing sound ever! Your washing machine has thrown a temper tantrum because of the way you treated it. It's letting you know in no uncertain terms that it is off-balance.

Our lives are like that. There are warnings that we are overloaded and, because of that, out of balance. And it is an awful thing. The results may not grab our attention in precisely the same way as the machine's warning buzzer, but the caution is just as real—in a different form. Nervous stomach—perhaps an ulcer. Your doc prescribes a mild tranquilizer or blood pressure meds. The stress has increased and your capacity to handle it has decreased. All this because you have the need to cause everyone to "rise up and call you blessed."

Dr. McBurney and his wife Melissa opened the Marble Retreat Center in Aspen, Colorado. He reported that one of the things he sought to do as he worked with clergy couples in crisis was to get them to accept that there was nothing they could do to diminish God's love for them. God's love for us begins with the fact of creation itself—God made us and loves us like our parents do, only more so. While we may know this *intellectually*, it may be hard to accept *emotionally*. Of course, the corollary that we desperately need to hear is that there is nothing we can do to *earn* God's love. We can't be good enough. We can't earn enough degrees or give enough money or leap tall buildings—again, in the goodness of God, we were born into this world, already possessing all the love from God we need to negotiate our way through life. So why is it, do you think, we can't seem to get it through our craniums that it isn't true that if we just get involved in doing more stuff, then others will respect us more and God will love us best?

Overachieving

In our culture, one of the best ways to earn respect from others is to achieve something significant. Almost everyone over the age of 50 cut their teeth on the adage, "work never killed anyone." Where I grew up, one of the worst labels you could ever be tagged with was "lazy!" And I went to great extremes as a youngster working on the farm to avoid that designation. (Uncle Ed, I don't care what you believe; I was not too young for my back to hurt while I was "thinning" corn on that hillside field!)

This is especially a problem for firstborns, who are generally overachievers in the family system, partly because they are hopeful for approval from the significant people in their lives. Although this characterization is certainly not limited to the eldest child in the birth order, this neurotic need to be liked together with the need to please the significant people in their lives—parents, spouses, the "boss," the "board"—have been heavy-duty, industrial-sized influences. And what better way to gain this status than to achieve?

In his first book, *Hide or Seek*, James Dobson discussed the various "coins" of worth attached to various people. He declared that beauty is the "gold coin," in our society, attaching worth to the less than one-tenth of one percent of the physically attractive people. He lists achievement as the runner-up to beauty, the winner of the "silver coin." In other words, invariably we attach value to others based on these two traits rather than regarding them as having inherent worth because God created them. The truth is that God creates us as persons of worth and dignity and there is nothing, not one blessed thing, we can do to earn it.

Typically, the American thing to do is work to be productive. Physician Richard Swenson, author of *The Overload Syndrome: Learning to Live Within Your*

Limits, reminds us that when productivity is overemphasized, the process is often perverted. We substitute work for faith, speed for substance or depth, money for love, and busyness for prayer.

Somehow we believe that being busy with the *things of* God is a suitable alternative for a *relationship with* God. We may cognitively accept that our frantic activity doesn't win "brownie points" with God, but our gut betrays us and we find ourselves attempting to do just that.

The apostle Paul writes in 2 Corinthians 7:1 that, "Since we have these promises, dear friends, let us purify ourselves from everything that contaminates body and spirit, perfecting holiness out of reverence for God." It's not a new idea—the mind and heart are integral components of the same system. Our bodies and minds interact so closely together that they keep catching each other's diseases! Certain contaminants affect our minds and bodies negatively—and one of them is hurry.

Workaholism

Another effect of hurry sickness is the problem of *workaholism,* the term Dr. Wayne Oates "invented" first in an article in the October 1968 edition of the *Pastoral Psychology Journal.* It soon became a household word in the United States and beyond in 1971 when his book *Confessions of a Workaholic* was published. He declares workaholism to be an addiction, much like an addiction to alcohol or drugs. In this case it is an "addiction to work, the compulsion or the uncontrollable need to work incessantly."

A workaholic is a someone "whose need for work has become so excessive that it creates noticeable disturbance or interference with . . . bodily health, personal happiness, and interpersonal relations, and with . . . smooth social functioning." As an admitted workaholic himself, Oates suggests that the illness is rooted in economic, cultural, and emotional deprivation one might experience in childhood. Regardless of its origin, it is clearly a colossal problem in our society.

I believe the terms "workaholic" and "hurry sickness" could be used interchangeably with ease. Look again at Dr. Oates's definition of a workaholic, substituting hurry sickness for work: "A person who is inflicted with [hurry sickness] is someone whose need to [hurry] has become so excessive that it creates a noticeable disturbance or interference with that one's bodily health, personal happiness, and interpersonal relations, and with that one's smooth social functioning." That is a classic definition, and it comes with an exacting price tag. Simply put, hurry sickness interferes with nearly everything that makes for the health and wholeness of one's life.

Impaired Judgment

One of the more serious costs of hurry sickness is the exercise of poor judgment. When we have the "luxury" of a quiet heart, a clear mind, and a rested body, we tend to have a greater capacity for making good, sound judgments. To put it another way, when our perspective is sound and our equilibrium balanced, we are able to draw conclusions more accurately and make decisions that are unencumbered by clutter and fatigue.

A hurried life often results in greater vulnerability toward making wrong decisions. The weariness that comes from an accelerated lifestyle blurs the distinction between right and wrong, and too often people choose paths that are counterproductive to emotional and spiritual wholeness. Fatigue reduces our critical faculties and clouds our pledge to the long-term commitments we have made and which enrich our lives. It becomes much easier, therefore, to allow impaired judgment to influence us toward impulsive decisions that will likely prove to be damaging to our best interests and the interests of others who are closest to us.

Technology has created an incredible panorama of opportunities to send and secure information in the blink of an eye. Individuals and organizations, business and non-business, have become dependent on computer systems. Once, the system in our shop crashed as a result of a virus that got through the firewall. No one knew what to do! We couldn't send or receive e-mail; we couldn't continue to work on word-processing documents; virtually everything we did was affected by the shutdown. People wandered the halls saying things like, "We might as well go home!"

But technology, while extraordinarily wonderful tools, may also be problematic, especially to persons who have addictive personalities (and most of us are addicted to something). Weariness can make people vulnerable to abuse of the very same technology that has been such a boon to business and industry. Someone might use the Internet in inappropriate ways and get hooked into emotionally and spiritually damaging behavior in the use of the Web. Most of us have heard stories of people who have formed cyber-relationships in chat rooms or with "instant messaging" that later proved toxic to them and other significant people in their lives.

Bewilderment

Bewilderment is part of the price tag for hurry sickness. The story is told that when Daniel Boone lived in southeastern Kentucky, he was often sought out as a guide by people who wanted to find their way through the mountains. Once he was guiding such a family through the Cumberland Gap. The folks in tow were amazed at the beauty of the area and the challenges presented by the terrain. Boone appeared to be not as familiar with that area. He went by himself over a hill, through a deep gap into a Kentucky "holler." When he returned, one of the men asked him, "Mr. Boone, have you ever been lost in these hills?" Boone replied, "Nope, never been lost—but I have been bewildered at times."

Bewilderment may come as a result of haste, and it sometimes occurs when you are ensnared by the need to make decisions between two good things. Life would be much easier if the decisions were between the clear options of good and bad. But that's not often the case for most of us. You would like to do everything, but you can't—you have to choose.

When we feel constantly hurried, we lose the deep sense of self-knowledge that helps direct us. We have no time for the slow thinking that most important life decisions require. Oddly enough, when we feel rushed and become bewildered, we procrastinate. (Can we talk about procrastination now, or would you prefer to put it off until later?) We put off making decisions but remain bewildered. You find your life confused and falling into disorder. The frantic activity around you has overwhelmed you, and you feel swallowed up by the disarray. In the most extreme cases, this becomes an ongoing way of living—we forget any other way. We have established a pattern of chronic rush that has removed the coherence from our lives.

Clutter

Clutter can be both a symptom and cost of hurry sickness. The late Thomas Merton, a Trappist monk, once wrote that our minds are like crows. They pick up everything that glitters, no matter how uncomfortable. What a great description of how clutter affects our lives!

Jogging never appealed to me. In fact, I never enjoyed the long-distance runs or some of the field events that are held at track meets. If you would ask what are the most exciting track and field events in the Olympic Games, my hunch is that the vast majority of answers would be the 100, 200, and 400 meter sprints, probably in that order. Watching a marathon, to me, is a lot like watching paint dry. Pole-vaulting is a lot more exciting than the shot put. And all that is very consistent with the "hurry" frame of reference, don't you think? We may admire endurance, but we are hooked on speed and swiftness.

Since I dislike jogging, I have taken up walking as a part of my exercise regimen. I do it every morning, all seasons of the year. I love getting up early and walking at 5:00 or 5:30 am. I walk fast, and the exercise over the two-mile course benefits me physically and mentally; but perhaps its greatest benefit for me is that it has become a time of prayer and meditation, a time to think through issues and plan the day ahead. (See, I can't just pray or meditate; I have to add thinking and planning.) Our neighborhood is hilly and a bit more settled than some places we have lived. There are young people, but we have not experienced much transition; people tend to stay when they move here.

One winter Saturday morning, I walked up the hill toward the end of our cul-de-sac, two-tenths of a mile to the end. On the way back, as light was breaking across the sky, and I began to notice discarded beer cans on both sides of the road. I counted a total of 29 beer cans strewn on both sides of the street. I mused that someone in my neighborhood, probably young someones with throbbing heads and mouths full of cotton, would soon be trying to remember how much fun they had the night before.

My immediate response was anger. I am a card-carrying, certified tree-hugger who believes in taking care of God's *oikos* (pronounced ee-kos). *Oikos* is the Greek word for dwelling place, house, household, family, and it implies stewardship or responsibility for management of a household. As one who believes that ecology is a more theological than political issue, I was mad! For some strange reason, my usually upbeat mood turned foul for most of the day. In all honesty, there were most likely other issues that bubbled up from just beneath the surface that day, but it was all triggered by the clutter. When our lives experience clutter of any type, be it discarded beer cans or other trash, it is hard to see God.

Kristin, our daughter, told me about participating in a silent retreat at the Gethsemani Monastery in

Trappist, Kentucky, where she and her family lived at the time. This is the same monastery where Thomas Merton lived and wrote. She told me of some books she had bought while she was there and recommended two of them to me, both by the same author, Joyce Rupp.

I ordered both books via the Internet and they were delivered to our home within the week. I was astonished as I started to read one of the books, *The Cup of Our Life: A Guide for Spiritual Growth*. One of the short chapters is entitled "The Cluttered Cup," and as I read it I was amazed that the author's experience with neighbor clutter was similar to mine. She wrote about many kinds of clutter: anxiety, resentment, harsh judgments, self-pity, and mistrust, and how they can take up so much inner space.

Rupp writes that anything can be clutter if it keeps us totally absorbed in ourselves and unaware that God is offering other gifts to us. Even the good things that come our way can be clutter when their acquisition and preservation require the investment of much of our psychic, emotional, physical, and spiritual energy. This, she writes, includes even prayer, the important practice that is intended to deepen our intimacy with God—even prayer can become a part of the clutter of our lives when it is regarded as a legalistic duty. When that happens, the practice becomes the focus rather than the relationship.

Clutter throws me off balance when I let it take over my mind or my emotions. There is not much room for

God's agenda when mine takes up all the nooks and crannies. Even prayer itself can become clutter if my spiritual practice becomes the focal point instead of my relationship with God.

As I read on, I recalled the wisdom of that pastor of my youth, "Brother" Oscar Byrd, who wrote in the Bible that Gatesville Baptist Church gave to me at my ordination: "God wants to give to all of us the greatest of all gifts; but we can't take them because our hands are too full of other things."

Other Costs

Undoubtedly there are other costs of hurry sickness that could be mentioned. Among them, one problem is anger—the kind that causes some hurried people to take awful, dangerous chances. For example, some of the more extreme cases of anger have resulted in road rage, sometimes ending in tragedy.

The U.S. Department of Transportation completed a study in the spring of 2002 that revealed the cities with the greatest traffic problems, including road rage. Much road rage is caused by extreme traffic conditions that turn the interstate highways in large cities into virtual parking lots. Washington, D.C. ranks third (behind Los Angeles and San Francisco), and I travel in that area several times a year. The report revealed that commuters spend almost 80 hours a year stuck in traffic. If that is a regular occurrence for you, then you understand the problem better than most.

Traffic near and on the Beltway is often so bad that it creates rage, never mind persons who are already mad when they get behind the wheel. I read that one person's idea of hell is to be caught in a Beltway traffic jam driving a sub-compact car, fronted by a diesel-belching bus, bounded on each side by two eighteen-wheelers racing their engines in stereo, and behind, a teenage hip-hopper driving a rolling boom box (the kind you feel as quickly as you hear it)!

Furthermore, depression, or anger turned inward, is often the result of hurry. Both anger and depression are characterized by a diminished ability to think clearly and creatively. The ability to do that is among the most important traits anyone can have in today's world. And the rush it takes to get through everything in record time eats away at that ability.

What about the physical costs? As already discussed, hurry is a leading cause of stress, and stress is a significant factor in the development of high blood pressure, increasing the chances for strokes and heart disease. Dr. Meyer Friedman, one of the cardiologists who coined the term "hurry sickness" almost 45 years ago, was alarmed at the similar patterns he saw in his patients. Some were overweight. Some were smokers. Others, though not obese, were hooked on the wrong kinds of foods for heart patients. But they all shared one characteristic with each other: chronic rush and the stress that came from it.

It is pretty clear that one of the things we value most in our culture is the importance of keeping things moving. Several years ago, before the new four-lane Willey Bridge had been built over the James River in Richmond, Virginia, the morning traffic would back up severely as the four lanes approaching the Huguenot Bridge (circa 1945) narrowed to two. Sometimes the backup would be almost a mile long, and everything would slow to a crawl. I noticed that some drivers started to turn onto streets on the right and left of Huguenot Road, presumably to "beat the rush" to the bridge. I also noticed that many of these cars arrived at the bridge at almost the same time as I, even though I had stayed in line.

One morning, I saw one of my coworkers take that detour. We stopped at a coffee shop and had our first cup of coffee for the day. I told him that I had seen him take the detour and wondered if he saved any time. My friend said to me that saving time really didn't matter that much to him; it just drove him nuts to sit in traffic! He would rather be moving because it gave him the illusion that he was making progress even it he wasn't.

Like Alice in *Through the Looking Glass*, we run furiously in order to stay in the same place. And like thousands of others, the cost to us physically, emotionally, and spiritually is enormous. We feed on pressure, personal challenge, and a full schedule. We always seem to need a full plate of some kind of activity or we either get restless or worse—we get bored. Addiction? You betcha! And like other addictions, we need to face it, own it, and get some help in order to deal with it.

Notes:

1. Archibald D. Hart, Ph.D., "Am I Too Tired?" *Christianity Today International/Leadership Journal* 19, no. 4 (Fall 1998): 31.

2. H. B. London, Jr. "Pastor to Pastor" audio tape series, vol. 12, narrated by Mike Trout (Colorado Springs, CO: Focus on the Family, 1994).

CHAPTER THREE

Prayer As Listening

*"There is vulnerability associated with listening...
where ... we may meet the unexpected
or the unwanted. The process of listening
is not always in our control and
what we hear may shake us up or wake us up."*
—Doris Donnelly in
Spiritual Fitness: Everyday Exercises for Body and Soul

*"Prayer catapults us onto the frontier of the spiritual
life. It is original research in an unexplored territory."*
—Richard Foster

Recently Lacey, my wife of more than forty years, accused me of *never* listening to her. At least, I *think* that's what she said. Fact is, most of us will have to plead guilty to occasional "functional deafness." We tend to hear what we really want to hear and filter out what we don't. This is an important trait, because if we were unable to do so, we would go bananas! The result is that we often miss something really important because this tendency generally means that we fail to develop good listening skills—either to others or to God. Thus what has been described as the most basic function in a relationship with God is fractionalized.

I was in a seminar when the leader was talking about prayer and how important it is to slow down enough to actually do it. After he had been talking for about half the hour he had been given to speak, he suddenly stopped his presentation and said to us, "Let us pray." After pausing for what seemed to be a full thirty seconds, he surprised us by saying, "Let us *not* pray!" He then proceeded to elaborate on what had just taken place. After he called us to prayer, everyone in the room bowed their heads, closed their eyes, and waited for the leader to pray.

Most of us have internalized this idea about prayer—that it is almost always in the form of a spoken word, words we speak to God. Even when we pray silently, we typically use words. But the reality is that prayer is a great deal more than words said either aloud or silently. Only in the past few years have I begun to understand prayer in other forms, such as listening. Listening to God can often be a more powerful and profound prayer experience than using words.

Some of us may have difficulty taking a contemplative approach to prayer, and not using words in prayer. The *Success Style Profile,* a widely used cognitive assessment instrument, has shown us that the majority of people in the U.S. are right-brained, conceptual, feeling-oriented, external persons. That, translated, means that most of us are generally uncomfortable with anything that is not moving. Action and activity are much preferred to inaction and inactivity. For many, "doing" is in first place of what it means to follow Christ, and nothing is second, not even prayer.

Many years ago I read a story about a young boy who lived on a farm and had never seen a circus. (I don't remember the source, but I think it is from one of Søren Kierkegaard's stories.) He learned that a traveling circus was coming to a town near his home, and he asked his father if he could go. His father gave his permission, provided the boy completed all his chores in time. When the lad finished his work, his father gave him some money, and he left for what he knew was going to be the most exciting event of his young life.

The boy arrived just before the traditional circus parade down main street was starting and he joined the crowds lining the street. He was not disappointed at the sight of it all. There were lions, tigers, elephants, monkeys, and all the other exotic animals that he had only heard about and had never seen.

When the clowns came along in their traditional position at the rear of the parade, flitting from one person to another, doing what clowns do to make people laugh and create interest, a very strange thing happened. When the last clown came by, the lad reached in his pocket and pulled out the money his father had given him, handed it to the clown, and left. The boy left for home, thinking he had seen the circus when he had only seen the parade!

In my view, this story describes in bold relief the problems we may encounter in our efforts to forge a relationship with God that is deeper than surface level. Many people don't pray much beyond the "now-I-lay-me-down-to-sleep" stage of spiritual maturity because they simply don't know how. The "protocol" of listening prayer is unknown to some, and their experience is not unlike the young boy who mistook the parade for the circus. But also like the lad, failure to learn these skills, so critical to a growing faith, means a stunted life, and a faith that is a pale imitation of the real thing.

North American Mission Board president Bob Reccord told the young theologues studying at New Orleans Baptist Theological Seminary that they should never confuse busyness with godliness. Good advice, that. One of his best lines was a quotation attributed to the acerbic evangelist, the late Vance Havner: "You can be as straight as a gun barrel theologically and as empty as a gun barrel spiritually."

Connecting Listening with Spirituality

I believe it is important to make a connection between the skill of listening with the whole idea of prayer and

Christian spirituality. While listening is a skill the techniques of which can be taught and learned, for the Christ follower, listening must be practiced in our relationship with God. It presupposes silence, and silence is far more than just the absence of the discordant sounds we usually define as noise. In fact, noise can *be* speech or sometimes even music. Someone once said that corn is a great crop, but even corn is a *weed* when it grows in a wheat field.

Kent Ira Groff, in his book *Active Spirituality*, points out that the formative word for the Hebrew community begins and ends with the *Shema* (she-MAH). It is the first word in Deuteronomy 6:4— "Hear [Listen!], O Israel: The LORD our God, the LORD is one." He says that *Shema* is the language of paying attention. The *Shema* was considered so critical to the solidarity of the Hebrew community that they were instructed to teach these words at home and away from home, when they lie down and when they rise (Deuteronomy 6:7).

The language of paying attention, paying attention to God, is so important that you should stop whatever it is you are doing in order to "pay attention." The meaning of this Hebrew word was picked up in the New Testament Greek word, *akouein* or *akouo*—again, to hear. It is the word from which we get the English word *acoustics*.

Both words mean more than simply hearing sound waves bounce off the walls. They mean to discern or to understand so that obedience may follow. Groff points out that the English *obey* is from the Latin root *audio* meaning "to listen beneath." Both the Hebrew and the Greek words for hearing are the same, "to listen beneath." Therefore, Groff says, "Contemplative prayer is training for 'listening from beneath'—to listen beneath the surface, to be attentive, to discern, to empty ourselves of our own prejudiced agenda. This kind of praying is training in holiness and wholeness."

On my first trip to China in 1995, I learned that the Chinese word for "hearing" or "listening" is a combination of four characters: *eye, ear, heart,* and *emperor.* This combination connotes how important "listening" is in the Chinese culture—important enough to listen as fully as one possibly can, using two empirical senses and one perceptive one. The addition of the word "emperor" adds credibility to the process of listening. That is, the emperor was revered to the extent that it was most important to do all that could be done to please him. In the case of believers, that "emperor" would be Jesus Christ.

Prayer and Spirituality: A Personal Journey

Many of us are a little suspicious of the idea of "spirituality"—we aren't sure there really is such a thing as *Christian* spirituality. And we are a little suspicious of techniques suggested to aid us in developing our spirituality. The fear seems to be that some of the practices related to spirituality seem, at best, a bit odd; at worst, New Age.

An intern for a religious newspaper here in Virginia wrote an article on the "labyrinth," a maze-like pattern which could be walked in prayer stages, and which was used by some churches and individuals as a tool for spiritual development. The response was immediate and in some cases harsh, with letters to the editor calling these churches to task for supporting something that was clearly "new age" and of pagan origins. Actually, the origins of the labyrinth are unknown, but Christians have been using them since the fourth century as a tool for meditation when seeking a closer relationship with God.

There is much about the subject of spirituality and prayer that is unknown to us, and we often fear looking very deeply into it. Or sometimes we just feel a profound discomfort when we try new things. During my time as a campus minister at Clemson University in South Carolina, we took our college students on a "silent retreat" at a nearby state park. Through that experience I learned how difficult it is for people to move "cold turkey" into a spirit of silence, solitude, and contemplation. Slowing down, quieting oneself, can be an abrupt change for those who aren't accustomed to the practice. The experience might be compared to detoxification from caffeine or some other substance— there is quite a struggle before you are able to calm down and readjust. Detoxifying your life from hurry, noise, and constant activity is difficult as well.

I led a Sunday school class at First Baptist Church of Clemson, which we jokingly referred to as the "Renegades Class." The class was made up of an interesting mix of professors, students, authors, and even one university president! We chose to study Richard Foster's book, *Celebration of Discipline.* When we got into the book, several class members decided they would like to actually practice some of the twelve spiritual disciplines Foster mentions in the book and make that a part of our study. Some focused on meditation; others, prayer. One couple, from a Mennonite background, chose fasting. Others decided to practice simplicity and solitude.

That study became transformational for many, including me. Because we lived in an academic community, the pace of our lives was increasingly rapid. Even in the early '80s it was a high-tech, high-volume world, and opportunities for quiet time were few. But it became clear that the disciplines in Foster's book were making an impact, especially the disciplines of silence and solitude.

One of the class members, in reflecting on the practice of silence, exclaimed on Sunday morning, "*Silence speaks!*" Ordinarily, that would have sounded a little like nonsense. But it is not, because silence has a different voice. It is still and small, like the experience of Elijah in the Old Testament that God doesn't necessarily speak in the whirlwind or in the storm. Mostly God speaks in that still, small voice that comes in silence. So the power of silence made perfect sense to all of us.

The Contemplative Life

While I was at seminary, I met a man at coffee break who really legitimized the whole idea of spirituality for me. I had not known many people who had addressed this subject directly prior to that encounter. Even though I had some level of comfort with this approach to the life of faith, I saw that there were weaknesses in my understanding. I wasn't clear how my spiritual practice might be nurtured toward maturity. That was where conversations with and the writings of Dr. Glenn Hinson entered center stage for me. Dr. Hinson, author of the Christian classic *A Serious Call to a Contemplative Lifestyle*, was a professor at that seminary, Southern Baptist Theological Seminary in Louisville, KY. I learned from him about the many spiritual resources that had not been a part of my experience because they were not familiar in my Baptist tradition.

That does not mean that they were not available to anyone. However, they were not always available to those of us in the evangelical tradition. The reason is connected to the Protestant Reformation of the 16th century. For many years, many of these resources were cloistered with the monastics of the Roman Catholic church. When the Protestant and Catholic churches separated, the newly emerging Protestants, under Martin Luther's leadership, assumed that prayer and spirituality were so essential to the Christian life that the resources would be brought out of their hiding places in the monasteries. Protestants brought the Bible out, but many of these resources on prayer remained within the Catholic church, and we are only just beginning to understand how these resources are enriching to our spirituality.

Toward Intimacy with God

Martin Luther himself clearly valued the importance of a deeply pious spirituality, and he continued to live the life of a monk even after the break with the Roman church, unrelenting in his desire to wear the monk's cowl. According to Roland Bainton in his classic book on Luther, *Here I Stand*, Brother Martin was an extremely busy person. He was a teacher, administrator, chaplain, and (most importantly, I think) a campus minister. But despite his schedule, he reportedly said that he would not have the time to do what he did if he did not pray the psalms for three hours every day!

Unquestionably Vatican II had a great deal to do with the new accessibility to these resources. Bill Moyers stated on one of his public television programs that had it not been for the Vietnam War, the sweeping changes in the Roman church spawned by Vatican II would have captured the headlines of the day. He suggested that Vatican II opened the windows of the Catholic church, and fresh winds were blowing through on a daily basis. The language and disciplines of spirituality, and various ways prayer is practiced may seem a bit odd to us, but not at all to the larger Christian church.

One of the principal proponents of opening the windows of the Catholic church was Thomas Merton, a Trappist monk who lived at the Gethsemani Monastery near Bardstown, Kentucky. Professor Hinson took one of his classes to observe the activities of the monastery and to discuss their significance with Merton, who was headmaster. After Merton had showed them around, they sat down to discuss their impressions. Dr. Hinson said that his original intention was to simply show the students a kind of "living museum"—he had not assumed that there would be much of an impact from the visit, either on him or the seminarians.

All the visitors, however, were very impressed with Merton's intellectual capacity and spiritual insights, and one of the students inquired why he would choose to waste his time in a cloistered place such as the monastery. Merton's reply was simple but profound: "Because we believe in prayer."

Dr. Hinson reported that this was a defining moment for him and most of the students because of the difference he saw in the two communities: the seminary and the monastery. At the seminary, prayer was discussed and its importance taught, but from a different perspective than how it was practiced at Gethsemani. At the seminary, developing a good devotional life was important in order to "do" something else. At the monastery, prayer was a means to nurture one's relationship with God. This, says Hinson, was a revolutionary understanding of the purpose of prayer.

The Best Reason to Pray

There is one best reason to pray and to listen to God as we pray. We pray because it nurtures our relationship with God—and that relationship is primary. Loyd Allen, professor of worship and spiritual development at Mercer University's McAfee School of Theology in Atlanta, teaches about prayer using a wonderful analogy. He asks us to imagine that he is a marriage counselor. He studies all the ways that he can be a successful marriage and family therapist. He sends his wife flowers and works to have a great relationship with her because he wants to be a good marriage counselor. But is there a better reason for him to do all those things for his wife? Of course—so he can be a better husband. Because he loves her. How many Christ followers desire a more intimate relationship with God in order to accomplish something else—being a better Sunday school teacher, a better witness, a better pastor, a better church member? When that happens, the relationship with God takes second place.

Have you ever wondered what your life would be like if you put God first in your prayer life? To actually begin and end there? If nothing follows that, if there is no by-product from prayer, might it be enough that you have been able to pull aside from the busyness of the day and to have discovered a deeper, more profound intimacy with the God of grace and peace?

The word "spirituality" is used in a variety of ways. It is almost impossible to define, but at least one way is to see it as a particular discipline or study that relates to our personal contact with God. The "disciplines" are those things within the Christian tradition that have proven helpful in fostering that personal relationship with God.

As we have already briefly discussed, one of the glitches in the actual practice of these disciplines is our own "holy impatience." Our religious tradition and our desire for action drive us to seek some tangible, measurable outcome for what we do. The idea that our relationship with God is important on its own, that the relationship isn't *for* anything but is crucial on its own, is difficult for us to see.

Again, Loyd Allen illustrated this in a profound way. He hypothesized that his wife, Libby, lives in one city and he lives in another. So he gets up every morning and calls her, breathlessly reciting a whole laundry list of issues and needs that are of great concern to him, without ever stopping or even pausing for a breath. He continues this inventory for twenty minutes and never pauses to allow Libby to say a word, signing off with, "I'll call you tomorrow. Bye!"

Then Dr. Allen concludes that his is a great marriage and decides that he will improve the quality of it by making another twenty-minute call to her that evening. He calls, talks another twenty minutes, again never pausing. What's wrong with that? The answer is clear. He is not listening!

In one of my seminary classes, the professor called on a classmate to open the class with prayer. The student started his prayer with, "Lord, as You read in the *Times-Picayune* this morning . . . ." My hunch is that this is the way most of us pray—a constant barrage of petitions, desires, information that we feel God may not be privy to and general statements about nothing much—never pausing long enough for God to speak to us. The reason? No one taught us to listen. Even during our silent prayer, we generally "talk." But we should realize that there is an intimacy with God that does not use words. There is a time to listen for God speaking to us. There is also prayer that is silence—just "being" in God's presence.

I have a platform rocker in a corner of my office that was a gift from my daughter. It is the rocker that was in our grandchildren's rooms when they were babies and one of my favorite things was to rock them to sleep for their naps and at bedtime. It is a "sacred" piece of furniture, and it occupies a sacred place in my heart (and my office). Often I get to the office a half-hour to an hour before the building opens. When I do, I go to that chair and attempt to center my soul before the start of a busy day. It helps me to remember that I used that rocking chair not only to get the grandchildren asleep but, in the process, to build a relationship with my grandchildren as we spent some special time together—certainly among the deepest and most important relationships of my life.

How do we do that with God? How might we keep that relationship alive and vital?

I grew up in Harrisville, Mississippi. There were not an overwhelming number of cultural activities available there, unless you count the Saturday night "tent" movies. There was no public school music teacher in our school. How much classical music do you think I heard in Harrisville?

In college my musical tastes broadened a bit, especially after I began dating the young woman who became my wife. She was earning an undergraduate degree in music (organ). When we were dating in college, I would occasionally go with her to the college's music history lab to listen to various classical compositions. The object was to become familiar with the composer, style, period, and other distinctive traits of the composition so that all this could be identified when the professor would drop the needle on the record at exam time. At first, it was not very enjoyable. Gradually, however, as I learned more about the composers and the music, I started to enjoy this music. I realized that it often seemed to give me what I needed: an emotional or spiritual lift, or a quieting of some inner turmoil.

Today, I prefer listening to classical music. Spiritual disciplines are like this. You may feel uncomfortable at first, but with practice and knowledge you find that they answer a soul-need you didn't know you had.

Since I grew up on a farm, we raised most of our food. The only things we bought at the store were staples such as sugar and flour. We even had our own corn meal ground at the mill. We were a vegetable, meat, and potatoes family—and meat only on Sundays when we had company (except for the bacon and sausage at breakfast). I had never tasted pizza until my first year in college, had never even heard of broccoli.

I still enjoy the foods I grew up eating. To me, nothing is better than fresh, vine-ripened tomatoes, fried okra, turnip greens, butter beans, crowder peas, and corn bread! But I am aware that there are other foods available to me now, and I love much of it. Whereas the food resources were once limited to what we had on the farm, now the resources have greatly expanded.

In like manner, all sorts of resources are now available to us from a variety of traditions. While our own "old time religion" might still speak to our heart in the most familiar, comfortable ways, other Christian practices can be learned and can greatly add to the richness and variety of our life in Christ.

The Seduction of Christian Spirituality

Ben Leslie worries that the resurgent interest in prayer and things spiritual may carry with it inherent dangers. A son of the Parker Memorial Baptist Church in Anniston, Alabama, and academic vice president and dean of the faculty at the North American Baptist Seminary in Sioux Falls, South Dakota, Leslie recognizes, as did St. Augustine centuries ago, that "no value is so good that it escapes the possibility of its own distortion." In his book, *The Seduction of Christian Spirituality*, he warns against the fallacy of casually dividing life into the spiritual and the physical, a kind of modern-day Gnostic approach to life.

He cites the late theologian Robert McAfee Brown's view that separating life into these two realms is a fallacy that excuses us from taking responsibility for the serious ethical problems that are so pervasive in modern society. He worries that preoccupation with the ethereal realm might preclude our engagement with the very real problems of the physical. Leslie quotes the pivotal passage in Micah, "What does the LORD require of you but to do justice, and to love kindness, and to walk humbly with your God?" (Micah 6:8 NRSV). He rightly contends that the verse is not a description of three separate kinds of activity, but three variations of a single theme. That is, the godly life is characterized by these acts of justice wherever justice is needed.

I believe that the significance of our ethical responses to human need will *increase* when they are linked to genuine biblical spirituality. Glenn Hinson suggested in *A Serious Call to a Contemplative Lifestyle* that because human beings possess a higher level of consciousness than others in the created order, we have a greater degree of ethical responsibility. The inward and outward dimensions of our Christian faith are really inseparable—you can't be right with one and wrong with the other. I have long contended that a lack of justice lies at the bottom of most of the world's problems. But a few years ago I started to realize an inner chaos in my soul that was more disconcerting than anything going on externally. No matter how hard I worked to "right the wrongs" in my small area of influence, I was not able to calm the internal roar created by seemingly unanswerable questions.

Not knowing precisely what the problem was, I sought the advice of a trusted friend who became a spiritual mentor to me. In the attempt to get to the root of "the dark night of my soul," we put everything on the table: the increased demands of my work, the frenzied pace of life, the emotional issues that created a measure of turmoil. Finally, after a few weeks, he observed to me that I was like a jar full of water and sediment of some sort, and the jar was all shaken up. He told me that he thought I could benefit from stillness and quiet so that the sediment could settle and the water could become clear.

My friend helped me to discover how to unplug, or disengage from the noise, the busyness, and the irregular rhythms of my life. After I had practiced this withdrawal for a few weeks, a strange thing happened: once again I started to become interested in the ethical issues and concerns that had driven me for so long. But I came to believe that this would not have occurred apart from the balance that was returned to my life.

We have already discussed how both the Hebrew and New Testament Scriptures point to such a balance in the very words used for "listen." Both *shema* and *akouein* connote obedience. To follow Christ's leading, we have to learn to "listen from underneath," to find a place of quiet and practice listening prayer so that our relationship with God can deepen. And Ben Leslie is right—when we do this, the results will be evident in our inner and our outer lives. We will not be split in two. A true biblical spirituality will not be seduced into an inner posture that has no corresponding outer reality. "Hear, O Israel: The LORD our God, the LORD is one." Listen! God desires us to live undivided, in oneness with God's Spirit.

CHAPTER FOUR

Getting Off the "Hurry-Go-Round"

" 'Tis the gift to be simple."
—Shaker hymn, origin unknown

An interesting story made the rounds in a recent email about people who seem to be obsessed with making sure that they are saddled up on the lead rodent in the rat race. As the story goes, a boat docked in a tiny Mexican village. An American tourist complimented the Mexican fisherman on the quality of his fish and asked how long it took for him to catch them. "Not very long," answered the fisherman.

"Then why didn't you stay out longer and catch more?" asked the tourist. The fisherman explained that his small catch was sufficient to meet his needs and those of his family. The American asked, "But what do you do with the rest of your time?" The fisherman replied, "I sleep late, fish a little, play with my children, and take a siesta in the afternoon. In the evenings I go into the village to see my friends, play the guitar, and sing a few songs. I have a full life."

The American tourist interrupted, "I have an MBA from Harvard and I can help you! You should start by fishing longer every day. You can then sell the extra fish you catch. With the extra money, you can buy a larger boat. With the extra money the larger boat will bring in, you can buy a second one and a third one and so on until you have an entire fleet of trawlers."

He continued, "Rather than selling your fish to a middleman, you can negotiate directly with the processing plants and maybe even open your own plant. You can then leave this little village and move to Mexico City, Los Angeles, or even New York City! From there you can direct your huge enterprise."

The fisherman asked, "How long would that take?" "Twenty, maybe twenty-five years," the tourist replied. "And after that?" "Afterwards? That's when it really gets interesting," answered the American, laughing. "When your business gets really big, you can go public, start selling stocks and make millions!"

"Millions? Really? And after that?"

"After that you'll be able to retire, live in a tiny village near the coast, sleep late, play with your children, catch a few fish, take a siesta every afternoon, and spend your evenings enjoying your friends!"

Pretty easy to see the irony in that story, isn't it? And yet I wonder if one of the major causes of hurry sickness may not be economic at its root. It's easy for us to buy into the "Great American Dream" of owning at least two sharp cars and living in as big a house as possible on our income. In many families, the kids are horrified if they can't buy their clothes at the trendy stores, and even Mom and Dad get caught up in this thinking. We feel we simply have to make more money to pay for the more expensive lifestyles—so we can finally reach a place where we have "enough" stuff to retire and enjoy life, like the fisherman in the story!

Have you seen the very funny film *The Jerk*, starring Steve Martin and Bernadette Peters? Steve Martin's character invented a device to help people avoid the trouble of using both hands to put eyeglasses on—and thus also prolong the life of the glasses. He made an enormous amount of money from this contraption and spent a lot of it very foolishly on his way out of poverty—mansions with swimming pools and beautiful gardens, servants, a collection of expensive cars, and other "toys" that showed he was *nouveau riche*.

Eventually his empire came crashing down when lawsuits were filed by many people who, when they used the device, had found it caused their eyes to cross! He lost it all. His wife was, of course, very glum about the whole thing. When Steve Martin apologized for losing all the money, her reply was classic: "I don't care about losing all the money—I just don't want to lose all the *stuff!*"

When we become devoted to "all the stuff," our lives become disordered—we are more likely to clutter our lives with way too much. Our days get cluttered, too. We have so many dates on our calendars that we feel strange and guilty when we aren't in a rush, juggling furiously to keep all the balls in the air. The big question is, once these patterns of acquisition and guardianship have been established, how do we disengage? It is hard to do, but I believe the process begins with the recognition that even a privileged lifestyle can leave certain basic needs unfulfilled. We need God to fill the emptiness brought on by the disappointing realization that the lead horse on the "hurry-go-round" leads nowhere.

'Tis the Gift to Be Simple

So—what must be done? As John Ortberg's friend asked: how do you ruthlessly delete hurry from your life? How about simplifying your life a bit—or a lot? Richard Foster writes in his book *Celebration of Discipline*, "Simplicity is freedom . . . Simplicity brings joy and balance . . . [freedom from] anxiety and fear." Have you heard this old Shaker hymn?

> 'Tis the gift to be simple,
> 'Tis the gift to be free,
> 'Tis the gift to come down where we ought to be,
> And when we find ourselves in the place just right,
> 'Twill be in the valley of love and delight!

The discipline of simplicity goes right to the heart of the problem of acquisitiveness. And it could be the most difficult discipline to get a handle on. For instance, have you ever vowed you were going to simplify Christmas this year, and found it impossible because of all the forces and expectations in your life? You can't disappoint your family, you need to reciprocate with friends who give gifts, you want to experience the beauty of the season—and you end up maxed out again. Some will even suggest it's unpatriotic to simplify, since the health of the American economy is dependent to a large degree on how successful merchants are during Christmas.

In order to simplify life, perhaps we should avoid the "cold turkey" approach and begin slowly. For example, how about finding one way to simplify Christmas? At Christmas time, my wife has begun sending contributions in the names of family members to Heifer International, an organization that offers hungry families around the world a way to feed themselves and to become self-reliant. They also teach farmers sustainable, environmentally sound agricultural techniques.

Of course, our two grandchildren, ages 9 and 6, have not yet learned what a joy it is to do something like this—but they will. The decision to simplify such celebrations is not easy, especially when family members gauge the success of the Christmas season by the number and quality of gifts they receive. But I would argue that Christmas gift-giving could be free of commercialism if families became intentional about these kinds of worthwhile gifts. And it would contribute significantly to relieving our hurry sickness.

Sleep as Spiritual Gift

Sleep or rest was identified briefly in the first chapter as one of the most spiritual things we can do. Resting well, in addition to helping us function as a Christ-follower, is also one of the best ways to jump off the "hurry-go-round." Sleep deprivation is being recognized as one of contemporary society's greatest problems. In the mid-nineteenth century the average American got 9.5 hours of sleep per night. By 1950, that had decreased to eight hours. Currently the range is from six to seven hours of sleep per night. Depending on the study, estimates range from 47 million to as many as 70 million Americans who are considered problem sleepers.

Some people take pride in being able to function on four to six hours of sleep, often wearing that claim as a badge of honor. But *every* time I have asked a group of young adults what they would do with an additional hour in the day, the answer has *always* been sleep! Our lives are moving with such increasing velocity that we are crashing in exhaustion. And we are getting sleepier and sleepier.

Dr. Richard Swenson, author of *The Overload Syndrome*, blames it on the invention of electricity and the light bulb. He rightly observes that we are a twenty-four hour society that seldom shuts down. Dr. Carl Hunt, director of the National Center on Sleep Disorders Research, concurs and adds that cable television, the Internet, email, and air travel exacerbates the already-serious problem of sleep deprivation. Jodi Matthews reported that the National Sleep Foundation's 2001 "Sleep in America" study revealed that a 24/7 society may offer endless opportunities for activities, but often at a great price: the encouragement of unhealthy and even antisocial lifestyles.

Lack of sleep has equally serious effects on the quality of life. When people do not get adequate sleep, 93% perform worse at work, 91% suffer more injuries, 44% have trouble getting along with people, and 25% eat more than usual, in some cases resulting in obesity and diabetes. If you go without sleep for more than a day, your performance is affected in the same way that an above-the-legal-limit alcohol level does.

Dr. Richard Parisi, director of the Sleep Disorders Center of Virginia, worries that as our lives get busier and busier, the increase in stress and depression grows significantly. The link between one's disposition and inadequate sleep is well documented, and the extent of harm is growing and appears to be a real "catch-22" situation: the stress that comes from busyness causes insomnia, and insomnia creates stress.

Here's the deal in a nutshell. Although the precise figures vary, most studies agree that many, if not most, of American adults are chronically sleep-deprived. There are many causes, some physiological. But many more are stressed and anxious, working more hours than ever before with a deep emotional investment in the "good life."

Technology, which was supposed to create more free time for us, has turned its ravenous appetite toward us and is consuming the time we do have. The blessings of technology are clearly there; but these blessings often have enslaved us as we become more addicted to them. As I write this, my cell phone is hanging on my belt, and my email system signals when I have incoming mail. That means that even when I am away from my office, I am never *really* away from my office, as long as I have these electronic umbilicals activated. We seem to feel that if we can just get more done, maybe we can have more stuff, and that will prove our worth, both to ourselves and to others. Like the cartoon in the New Yorker magazine in my doctor's office (a 1988 edition), "We have gotten to the top but have discovered the ladder is leaning against the wrong building."

Day Is Dawning—Or Not

When does a day begin? Seminary professor Stephen Brachlow led a retreat I attended recently. The theme focused on the importance of Sabbath to our experience of intimacy with God. Brachlow reminded us that the whole idea of rest has its basis in the creation story in Genesis 1. After each creative act—the creation of day, night, sky, dry ground, and so on—the narrator pauses to announce that a day has come and gone, that the evening and the morning were the first day . . . the evening and the morning were the second day . . . and the third, fourth, fifth, and sixth day.

Brachlow said that this order is no accident, that the Hebrews ordered life around a day that started with the evening rather than the morning. This is seen most clearly in the Jewish observance of the Sabbath, which begins at sundown on Friday and ends at sundown on Saturday. The theological idea is that God begins working in the evening, the conventional time for sleeping. God's activity continues through the night, and we awaken in the morning to join God in that activity. Henry Blackaby popularized this idea in *Experiencing God*—namely, that one of our major tasks is to find out what God is doing and join God in it.

Our fast-paced culture ought to pay attention to the wisdom of Genesis here. Seeing the day beginning at evening teaches something essential about who we are as human beings—that this sequence conditions us to the rhythms of grace—God begins working when we sleep. Eugene Peterson says that when he quits his day's work, nothing essential stops—that he goes to sleep *to get out of the way for awhile.* And that gets him into the rhythm of salvation.

Martin Marty, the Christian author/teacher, jokes that his Swiss ancestry gives him a special way with time and recommends *napping* to boost energy and productivity. He reports that for many years on most days he has taken two naps every day. He counsels those who have difficulty slumbering that "what keeps us awake and stressful is guilt about yesterday and worry about tomorrow."

Sabbath. Rest. Salvation. One of the most spiritual things anyone can do is to get quality sleep. As a work colleague said, sleep is an act of relinquishment and trust. Sleep as "sacrament" infers that you are going to leave the world's troubles to God for a period of time while you rest, that God may be able to do without your efforts for at least one night. Whatever it takes to accomplish this should be done. And then we awaken to the "steadfast love of the LORD [that] never ceases, his mercies never come to an end; they are new every morning" (Lamentations 3:22–23a NSRV).

Spaces in Your Togetherness

One of the most popular quotations in wedding cere-
monies is from Kahlil Gibran's *The Prophet*: "Be
together . . . but let there be spaces in your together-
ness." The implication is that healthy relationships
flourish when each person gives the other his or her
"space." Swenson calls it "margins," but the idea is the
same. When narrowed expectations are imposed for
whatever reason, it has a binding effect. Healthy relationships are built on trust, and the fundamental
nature of trust is not in its bind but in its bond.

Henri Nouwen said in an article in *Leadership Journal* (Spring 1985): "In the spiritual life, the word *discipline* means the effort to create spaces in which God
can act." Our busyness may severely restrict those
spaces. Further, it reduces our focus to the point that
we lose much of our capacity to be "present" to the
need that surrounds us. Preoccupation becomes our
modus operandi for just about everything we do in our
lives.

For example, how many times have you misplaced
your car keys? You *know* you placed them on the coun-
tertop when you came in with a load of stuff from
the office. And when you need to leave for an appointment in twenty minutes, they are *not* where you left
them. You launch a frantic, full-scale search, throwing
a steely-eyed, accusatory glance toward your spouse—
a "you-must-have-picked-them-up-and-hidden-them-

somewhere" look—and on your third trip upstairs, you reach into your coat pocket and . . . there they are.

I have learned to carry my cell phone with me into the grocery store because it is easier to call my wife than to remember to take a list . . . and I do that an average of twice on about every trip. It makes her very happy that I want to talk with her so often.

Again, Jesus is our best example. He never seemed to be in a hurry about anything. On the night before He died, Jesus made an astonishing claim: "I have brought you glory on earth by completing the work you gave me to do" (John 17:4). Completed? With all the serious needs of the dozens of people, He can say that His ministry is completed in a scant three years? What is He thinking?

The Gospels reveal that Jesus was, in fact, busy about God's work. But while His ministry could be characterized by a great deal of activity, it was never frenzied and He was never frazzled. It was clear that He took time for people and that He was joyfully and fully present to each. Think of Jesus' experience with the Samaritan woman at the well in John 4, or with Zacchaeus in Luke 19, or when He was urged to go to Judea and Jesus replied that the time (*kairos*) had not yet come (John 7:1–9). Do you feel Jesus rushing? I don't.

A.E. Whiteman observes that Jesus' understanding of His purpose gave an air of leisure to His crowded life, in his book *The Discipline and Culture of the Spiritual*

Life. What was Jesus' secret? We get a fairly reliable idea from Mark 1:35: "Very early in the morning, while it was still dark, Jesus got up, left the house and went off to a solitary place, where he prayed." The secret to Jesus' busy but balanced life was His *intimacy* with God. And this critical relationship gave to Him the ability to understand His human limits and to accept the boundaries as a fully human person so that He was able to resist the urgent demands of others.

Spirituality as Duty

Randy Wright, a friend who is a pastor in South Carolina, participated in a residency in "spiritual direction." In a recent discussion I had with him about his experience, he commented that he no longer talked about spiritual formation in terms of spiritual *discipline*. Rather he preferred to think of this process as spiritual *rhythms*.

Although we will use the terms *rhythms* and *disciplines* interchangeably, that concept is very instructive, especially in a religious culture that places a great deal of importance on the "mustness" or "oughtness" of one's spiritual life—for instance, one *must* have a quiet time, or you *ought* to keep a journal to record the experiences of your spiritual life, or you *must* pray daily in order to deepen your walk with God. While these "musts and oughts" hold a kernel of truth, they may become counterproductive when our spiritual practice becomes more compulsive performance than a free expression of gratitude.

The culture of American life is characterized by hurry and busyness. There is little we can do about that. All of us are subject to the rapid pace of our day. Unless you are a hermit or are involved in some cloistered religious order, it is almost impossible to focus with laser-like intensity on prayer, meditation, silence, and solitude. The result is that such "efforts" are probably doomed to failure—accompanied by the guilt that usually walks hand-in-hand with such failure—precisely because they are *primarily* efforts rather than an overflow of a graceful life.

Therefore, it seems to me that the goal is *balance*, or in the language of systems theory, *homeostasis*. *Homeostasis* may be defined variously as "equilibrium," "stability," "steadiness," "aplomb," and "uniformity." According to Ed Friedman, author of *Generation to Generation*, systems thinking assumes that regardless of one's quirks, "if the system exists and has a name, it had to have achieved some kind of balance in order to permit the continuity necessary for maintaining its identity."

What happens when the systems of spirituality get out of balance? Well, what happens when the tires on your vehicle get out of balance? The ride is both rough and often noisy—and if balance is not restored soon, you will suffer not only the indignity of a rough ride but a costly one as well when you replace the worn tires with a set of new ones.

Friedman further suggests that when a thermostat controls the temperature balance in a house, it is done within a *range*; it is not an inflexible point. Therefore, the notion of one's spiritual *rhythm* makes perfect sense in the attempt to forge a more intimate connection with God. It is critical that we are able to understand the rhythms of a busy life. They are mostly irregular in nature. There is little about the dailiness of life that is fixed or static.

I know pastors who define what they do as a "ministry of interruptions." They are constantly interrupted, and that's where they often find ministry opportunities. Time management gurus talk a lot about how the efficient use of time is in direct proportion to the ability to manage interruptions effectively.

Understanding that, we need not feel paralyzing guilt when we fail to perfectly observe the classical spiritual disciplines of silence and solitude, prayer and meditation. The fear that God is somehow deeply disappointed in us, or worse, is angry with us because we are "just average" Christians can inhibit us from moving nearer the warming fires of God's love and grace.

Richard Foster contends that the disciplines of the spiritual life are not merely for spiritual giants. Rather, the classical spiritual disciplines (classical because they are central to experiential Christian faith, he says) are for ordinary people who have to fight rush hour traffic to get to work, have mortgages and car payments, and juggle all the activities of their children—people with all the problems and privileges of life today. Foster writes in *Celebration of Discipline*, "If [these disciplines] are to have any transforming effect, the effect must be found in the ordinary junctures of human life."

Foster stresses, however, that one way to eliminate the effectiveness of such disciplines in one's personal life is to see them in their "oughtness." For these spiritual rhythms to be most helpful, we must avoid falling prey to legalism as we practice them.

In the Sermon on the Mount (Matthew 5:1; Luke 6:17), Jesus taught that in order for our righteousness to exceed that of the scribes and Pharisees (Matthew 5:20), we must avoid falling into a Pharisaic style of righteousness that focuses on manipulation and control rather than on freedom and grace. For "when the Disciplines degenerate into law, they are used to manipulate and control people." Living in the tension between the irregular rhythms of busy lives and the desire for deeper spiritual development sometimes exposes us to the burden of managing others' lives. When that is the case, the trip from grace to law is a short one. And our freedom to experience God in God's fullness is weakened.

Nurturing Silence in a Noisy World

In the book *Nurturing Silence in a Noisy Heart,* Dr. Wayne Oates discusses the problem of functioning in a noisy culture. He asserts that our very hearts are "noisy arenas" and, referencing the old hymn *Just As I Am,* points to the noise of our "fightings within and fears without." These noises, says Oates, drain our strength and sense of direction. The idea of silence in the midst of such noise is a happy prospect for many who hunger for it.

As a good friend reminded me, there are other noises that test our tolerance. Some of them are literal noises and reflect a society busily engaged in work and play. Even good things may sometimes become noise to us. Generally we enjoy listening to good music on the car radio—it helps us pass the time as we travel. But there are times when even the sounds coming from the radio become noise, especially when there is a deeply-felt need to clear the channels of our minds in order to be able to hear what God may be trying to say to us.

That's one kind of noise, however, that you and I can control. Perhaps it would be more fruitful to run counter to the old southern gospel song. Rather than "turn the radio on and listen to the music in the air," it might be better actually to turn the radio *off* in order to get in touch with God. And thereby dismount the interminable hurry-go-round.

CHAPTER FIVE

In Search of a Well-Ordered Life

"It is not enough to have a good mind.
The main thing is to use it well."
—Rene Descartes

The mother of a large family took one of her seven kids to the dentist to have a broken tooth fixed. The dentist examined the child and told the mother that he could find no problem with her teeth. The obviously harried mother looked at the dentist in disbelief and then looked at the child and exclaimed, "Oh, my goodness, I've brought the wrong kid!"

That story is not too great a stretch in a culture that has elevated speed as one of its highest values. Do you know what the fastest-growing sport is in this country? Stock-car racing. Why should we be surprised that a busy mother with seven kids might make the mistake of taking the wrong one to the dentist? Stranger things have happened.

Speed. Haste. It is clear that if we are devoted to something that is so clearly pathogenic, or sickness-causing, we will never find our way to well-ordered lives that confess the beauty of God's peace. Those of us who suffer from hurry sickness often strive very hard to have well-ordered lives. We think that order will help us accomplish more in less time! Organization, list-making, efficiency planning—all good things on their own—only increase our problem when we use them to feed our hurry sickness.

Have you ever met someone who you felt had a truly well-ordered life? If a person is serene, unhurried, gracious, organized, and rested, we often think they "have it all together," or have a well-ordered life. Many of us believe that money can buy a well-ordered life, because you can pay someone to rush around and do things for you. This is only a superficial reality. What is a true well-ordered life?

A well-ordered Christian life is simply one in which God's Kingdom is evident. In the same way that a person in charge can straighten up a household or a business, God's rule orders a life so that it is nourished, productive, healthy, and rightly ordered. God's Kingdom influences our large and cataclysmic life decisions as well as the small interior decisions no one sees. What is seen is the result—a life ordered by God. You know it when you see it.

A truly well-ordered life cannot be achieved apart from God's rule. All the plans, business models, organizational systems, and health regimens in the world cannot do for us what God wants to do in our lives. God's knowledge of us is perfect, God's will for us is specific and personalized, and God's presence with us is constant. We are only well-ordered if God orders our lives.

Given these truths, why would anyone not want God's rule in their life? I believe it is because we have gone wrong. We don't even have sense enough to want the right things. Hurry sickness is a small part of the larger disorder of sin—our desires have gone wrong, and they lead us in the wrong direction.

Saint Ignatius Loyola said the goal of spiritual exercises was to "free people from disordered affections." In other words, spiritual disciplines help the Christ follower to love the right thing to the right degree with the right kind of love. Ignatius used a method of daily devotion, known today as the Ignatian Examen, to develop in his community a discerning way of life in order to practice that kind of love. Noticing and becoming aware of God's presence daily requires an ongoing practice that illumines one's life with the light of God. (Christians of all kinds, Catholic and Protestant, have found the Ignatian Examen to be a helpful spiritual practice for listening for God's guidance. I highly recommend that you get some information about it and try it!)

Creating Margins

If we are ever to cope adequately with the stress brought on by overload, we must learn to create "margins" in our lives. The term "margin" may not yet be a household word, but its importance cannot be overstated. It is a term coined by Dr. Richard Swenson, a physician who is a professor at the University of Wisconsin School of Medicine. In his book *The Overload Syndrome,* he defines *margin* as the space that exists between our load and our limits.

As a physician, Dr. Swenson has seen a steady parade of exhausted people march through his office. They came with a variety of physical symptoms, but most of them had one common characteristic: their loads were too great and their boundaries too narrow. In other words, there were no margins in their lives.

Margin is something held in reserve for contingencies or unanticipated situations. It is the gap between breathing freely and suffocating under the load brought on by the simple everyday nature of our hectic lives. It is manifested by stress, fatigue, and anxiety.

Every facet of our lives is affected, especially relationships. And much of it is brought on by our addiction to hurry. Think about your life. Do you have a sense that there are margins there? Imagine you had a flat tire in the morning, or you were sick for a few days—do you immediately feel a sense of anxiety or fear about it, that too many things would go undone, too many parts of your plan would be thrown off? You might need to build more margins in your life.

Others have made many good suggestions about ways to a well-ordered life. I will focus in this chapter on just two of what I consider to be the greatest and most *subtle* challenges of the well-ordered life: the special problem that interruptions bring and the whole area of dealing with the "information glut."

The Ministry of Interruptions

Have you ever wondered how Jesus was able to maintain such perfect balance in His life? It's too easy to say that it is because He was both perfect man and perfect God. While it is true, that belongs to mystery. The Bible teaches that the real miracle of the Incarnation is that God became *human* and lived as fully as possible into what that means—that the humanity of Jesus infers no special "advantage" over other humans—that, in fact, Jesus was "in every respect . . . tempted as we are, yet without sin" (Hebrews 4:15b RSV).

What's the difference, then, between the feverish way in which our lives are often lived and the "non-anxious" presence of Jesus? Perhaps one of the best answers to that question is found in the story of the healing of the paralytic man whose friends let him through the roof on a stretcher (Mark 2:1–12). I owe the inspiration of this idea to the late Eddie Freeman, who preached a sermon in the 1980s on the subject of how Jesus handled interruptions, based on Mark 2:1–12.

I find the language of the Authorized Version very instructive: "and it was *noised* that he [Jesus] was in the house" (Mark 2:1 KJV). "Noised" is most likely an accurate description—because apparently the crowds had gathered around the house, ten-deep on all sides, foreclosing the possibility of any normal entry into the house. How the four men bearing the paralyzed man on the stretcher got to the rooftop is a bit of a mystery given the crowds. Nonetheless the act revealed the depth of their friendship and commitment, and they proceeded to build the first open-air skylight known to Middle Eastern architecture.

Given the circumstances of this story, it is easy to miss an important point, maybe two: (1) apparently it was the quality of the faith of these friends that made the difference here. "Because of *their* faith," the Bible says, never mentioning the faith of the sick man; (2) Jesus was unperturbed by the interruption. The second point is the most intriguing to me, and Jesus' grace and sensitivity in handling this intrusion is extraordinary.

What was there about Jesus—who got hungry when He went without food, who experienced pain when He hit his thumb with a hammer, who became tired after dealing with multitudes of people—what created His capacity to be unaffected by this shocking disturbance?

I was in a worship service once when a troubled young man rose to challenge the preacher about something that was said, and the congregation was totally shocked. Apparently the preacher was the most shocked of all because he had been "on a roll" (as we say in the trade), but he never recovered his momentum. That's often the way it is with interruptions.

Think about it—when I am trying to preach, I get frustrated when the cutest-baby-in-the-world is making eyes at the people in the pew just behind the cherub; and when the same baby lets out a blood-curdling yelp, I do my best to ignore it and move on, but it can get a bit frustrating. I wonder what my reaction would be if suddenly the ceiling started dropping, and someone was lowered from the roof through the ceiling joists to the floor of the sanctuary. (Would never happen in my case because the throngs who come to hear me preach are *seldom* ten-deep around the church.)

I think it is reasonable to assume that Jesus was interrupted a lot. And we need to remember that He didn't have the luxury of an administrative assistant who screened calls and guarded her boss's time. There are snippets of information indicating that some of those closest to Jesus sometimes tried to protect Him from others, as when Phillip and Andrew detained some Greeks who wanted to see Him (John 12:20–28). But most of the time nothing seemed to obstruct open access others had to Jesus. It is clear that Jesus understood the value of the rhythms between work and leisure. But it is noteworthy to me that there is nothing in the Scripture that even implies that Jesus ever became impatient with those who were "given" to Him during the course of a busy day.

Therefore, in Mark's account of the incident, this constancy remains. There is no outburst against these intruders that they were interrupting the worship of God, no railing toward these misguided zealots. On the contrary, Jesus turned His full attention to the men who cared enough for their friend to risk the wrath of the Messiah as well as those in attendance. And He forgave and healed this man, telling him to "take your mat and walk."

I find the sequence of that incident very fascinating. (Apparently the scribes did also.) That He *forgave* the man his sins before He healed him shows the depth of His concern for him. It occurs to me that He could have healed the man and quickly returned to the service. But Jesus took the time to address even deeper spiritual needs as He dealt with the physical. I wonder what I would have done. I probably would have been eager to get the healing done and these "intruders" on their way.

But not Jesus. Again, what strikes me is the quality of attention Jesus gave to these men. Gerard Egan authored *The Skilled Helper,* a textbook on counseling still used in many undergraduate and graduate programs. One of the primary theses of the book deals with three levels of a counselor/therapist's capacity to perceive a client's "situation" accurately. The first level is the most basic: *empathy,* when whatever takes place between the client and counselor is focused on building trust.

As the client reveals or "self-discloses" beyond the initial opaqueness of the their time together, the counselor is able to perceive issues at the second stage: *accurate empathy.* The highest level of perception, according to Egan, is *advanced accurate empathy,* a stage where the therapist has successfully communicated "unconditional positive regard" toward the client. At this point, the client trusts the therapist at such a deep level that the therapist can truly help the client.

Such helping requires that the counselor be able to deal with his/her own internal "stuff." Because counselors are human, they are beset with human problems, some of which are serious enough to affect their work by preventing them to be fully and joyfully present with others. This was not a problem with Jesus, however, as demonstrated by the way He handled such intrusions. As a friend said, Jesus was able to respond positively to such human need because He "had Himself off His own hands" and could give His complete attention to whoever was placed in His path.

Because Jesus' life was balanced, He never felt the need to rush. Rather, He dealt freshly and attentively with everyone. This kind of unhurried devotion was transformational in every situation. If I am always skittering about, captive to the rapid pace of daily life. If I am too busy or too preoccupied with my own agenda to attend the intrusions that are part of my life, the chances are good that I may be missing many of the blessings God sends through others.

What if the primary focus of a person's life and ministry were measured in the way they handle interruptions? Suppose that *is* our ministry, and everything else we do is less important than what we do when we are interrupted. If, in fact, God is present to us in Jesus Christ, maybe that *is* the basic way we should live—that life itself consists of being fully present to everyone and everything that comes within the range of our vision—even the interruptions.

What a way to function! What a way to develop a well-ordered life—by adopting the non-anxious presence so clearly demonstrated by our Lord. He had to have experienced an unending series of intrusions, yet the comfort He had in His own skin, His understanding of life itself, connected with His sense of grace sustaining it all, gave Him the balance that shines throughout the pages of the Gospels. Jesus always responded with *joie de vivre*, with lively exuberance, because He saw God's fingerprints on everything, even on some men ripping a hole in a roof during worship. This is the way

He responds to you and me as well!

Don't you hate it when telemarketers call around dinnertime? Our daughter even had a snippy little message just for them: "If you are a telephone solicitor, please leave your home phone number and we'll return your call at dinner time." Is that tacky? Most don't think so because of the number of times dinner has been interrupted by someone using the phone to sell something or to conduct another survey. When the "niceness gene" kicks in, the obligation some people feel to answer every call is both undeniable and overwhelming.

But I wonder—what if we took the time to be cordial to these folks who most likely have had to endure the "slings and arrows" of an annoyed public pretty much all day for minimum wage? What if we just didn't get too worked up about a child who interrupts Tom Brokaw just when the evening news is showing something we didn't want to miss? What if we could put aside whatever it is that we are doing to talk with a colleague or friend who drops by to visit? What if we deliberately drove our cars in the slow lane to let the guy in a behemoth SUV get in front of us? What if we got in the long line at the grocery store and let others slip in line ahead of us? (Probably be wise to check with the guy behind us before you do that, however. His "niceness gene" may not have been activated yet.)

What if we could live with the same sense of grace and tolerance for the intrusions of the day, seeing them as vehicles delivering blessings rather than frustrations? What if . . .? What if . . .?

I am writing this while visiting my ailing father, 87, in Mississippi. He is suffering from a variety of disorders, including blindness (for about the past six years). His most serious problem, however, is an Alzheimer's-like dementia, called Multi-Infarct Dementia (MID). It occurs when blood clots block small blood vessels in the brain and destroy brain tissue. Several neurological symptoms exist, including stroke, dementia, migraine-like headaches, and psychiatric disturbances.

My dad wandered into my room one day in one of his rare, lucid moments. He told me that he was sorry he didn't recognize me at the breakfast table earlier and that he, in fact, was ashamed that he didn't know his eldest son. I assured him that I understood and that he should not worry about that. We talked about several things, mostly people in the "old days," but also about death, especially his own. I said to him, "Daddy, you have lived a long, happy, and productive life, and I know you are spiritually prepared to face the next life." He responded, "Yeah—I'm ready to go—but I don't want to leave yet." I was glad he couldn't see well enough to notice the tears flowing down my face. I will remember the moment for the rest of my life. It was a wonderful interruption, and I could just as easily have missed it.

Information Junkies versus a Well-Ordered Life

One of the byproducts of the technological age is increased flow of information. One of the constants of the corporate world is change. For years, change occurred incrementally, and the business world had the luxury of planning in advance, because the changes happened slowly. Now, change moves exponentially. And of course, such rapid change leaves little time for long-range planning. More than one corporate executive said that success would be measured by speed of access to the most information.

Jeff Davidson, a management consultant, speaker, and educator from North Carolina, wrote in *The Complete Idiot's Guide to Managing Time* that tackling new information is like drinking from a rain barrel. Suppose you were tremendously thirsty and the only way you could satisfy your thirst was to lift a rain barrel and try to sip the water. First, it would require extraordinary strength and balance. But there might be a better way. You *could* take a small cup, dip it in the barrel, and remove the water a few ounces at a time.

There is a similarity between trying to gulp water from a rain barrel and taking in the huge load of information that assaults us every day. We are constantly bombarded with information from every conceivable place, and when we try to take in and process everything that's hurled our way, the result is like drowning.

There are two approaches to the information glut that need to be discussed if we are going to get serious about reordering our lives. One, how might we reduce the overabundance of information we receive? Two, what can we do to reduce *our own contribution* to the problem?

Drowning in Information

Did you know that, according to the *Native Forest Network,*

- The majority of household waste consists of unsolicited mail?

- 100 million trees are ground up each year for unsolicited mail?

- 28 billion gallons of water are wasted each year for paper processing?

- More than half of unsolicited mail is discarded unread or unopened and the response rate is less that 2%?

- The result is more than 4 million tons of paper waste each year?

- This paper is hard to recycle, as the inks have high concentrations of heavy metals?

- $320 million of local taxes are used to dispose of unsolicited mail each year?

- It costs $550 million annually to transport junk mail?

- The growing landfills disfigure rural areas and pollute ground water?

- We get about 40 pounds of junk mail a year, more than a tree's worth per family?

These basic facts, along with general guidelines and tips on getting rid of junk mail, spam, and telemarketers are found on the EcoFuture web site, www.ecofuture.org. To tree-huggers like me, this is startling information that should give pause to anyone who is concerned about the stewardship of the resources God has allowed us to use.

When you receive information, you have to respond to it somehow—even if only to delete unwanted email. When you get too much flung at you, it is easy to get the overwhelming feeling that others have too much control over your time.

Restructuring Our Action-Filled Lives

A well-ordered life requires that we adopt Jesus' style of handling the intrusions that come our way all the time. It also demands that we know how to deal creatively and positively with the flood of information hammering us daily. These reactions require Christ-like love. But how do we love the right thing to the right degree in the right way with the right kind of love?

Perhaps the first order of business in that task is to find a way to deal resourcefully with the problem of time. I suppose it would not be too difficult to characterize this book as a work on time management. To the extent that it is clearly impossible to increase awareness of God and of others when our own lives are shredded into the tiny fragments of out-of-control time, I suppose it is. However, as Dorothy Bass teaches in her book *Receiving the Day*, we need to develop a language that is richer than the language of management. "We need to develop the patterns that get us through our days not only with greater efficiency but also with greater authenticity as human beings created in God's image."

Living a well-ordered life is more than just managing our time. But ordering our time commitments plays a huge role in helping us become an authentic Christ follower. I want to make two suggestions that will, if practiced intentionally and consistently, bring balance to our action-filled lives. Obviously there are other good suggestions, but I would argue that the majority of them are rooted in these two.

1. Prioritize your promises.

One of the worst mistakes we make is spending time on concerns or issues that are not true priorities. Nothing weird or revolutionary here. Quite simply, assign A, B, or C to your list of tasks. Work on the A priorities first, moving to the B priorities as you get to them. Then put the C priorities on the back burner and forget them. If they become more important, they will notify you on the way up.

For example, my wife once wanted me to paint the bathroom. In terms of my skills and inclination, that was a C priority for me. But as the days went by, she would say to me, "You know, that bathroom really needs painting," followed a few days later by, "I really wish you would paint that bathroom this weekend." Or, "Say, have you noticed how Kelly is eating the paint chips falling from the ceiling of the bathroom?" Suddenly, the C priority has become an A priority! My marriage depends on whether or not I paint the bathroom! It "notified" me of its increasing importance as it rushed up the priority scale.

2. Learn how to say *no* gracefully to good things.

I have to come clean and acknowledge that this is the issue I struggle with more than any other. And it often gets me in trouble. This probably never happened to you—but someone honors me by asking me to do something, sometimes six months to a year in advance. I look on my calendar and see that I have that date open. In fact, I have the whole month open! So, because I need to be needed, I say yes. Then, as the time approaches, I look at my calendar again and ALL the dates have filled up around the one original one, and I find myself wondering, "Why did I say I would do that?"

Saying no is not a test of orthodoxy. In fact, it may be the best way to allow God to work in us. Thomas Kelly, in his classic book *A Testament of Devotion*, urges us to rise above the need to manage others' lives and to center our lives not on the temporal but on what truly lasts. He reminds us, *"No* as well as *yes* can be said with confidence."

When we are able to say no, we create space in our lives for God to work. We are not blown about by every shifting wind, or by the plans of others. We are able to accept the interruptions that God sends our way calmly and warmly, in the spirit of Jesus. We are able to welcome God's priorities.

Our lives are only well-ordered when God's desires for us are on our A list. What a relief it will be for us when that happens! We could never have truly succeeded using the world's standards, because they are ultimately unsatisfying and the rewards aren't worth it.

Do you desire a well-ordered life? Don't worry about the state of your closet, or your household paperwork, or even your Day-Timer. Ask God to show you what are A, B, and C priorities in your life. Trust God to know what's right and to help you. And let your anxiety and hurry sickness go.

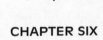

CHAPTER SIX

Waiting on God

"Be still before the LORD and wait patiently for him."
—Psalm 37:7

We appear to live in a culture that conspires to force all of us to move through life as quickly as possible. Some of the devices that are designed to carve out more personal time and to quiet our minds actually have the opposite effect. Our world is speeding faster and faster. And there are few, if any, off-ramps.

Sue Monk Kidd is one of the most honest writers I know. She coined the word "quickaholic" in a wonderfully candid book on spiritual direction called *When the Heart Waits*. She discusses in a very fresh way that we are so seduced by the need to secure instant results for just about everything that our capacity to wait has been severely eroded. We might wish that the pace of life would slow down, but we really hate to wait. It seems such a waste of time to us, and time is precious when you're always in a hurry.

It's true for me. I sometimes get the oil changed in my car at Jiffy Lube, because they will do it quickly. Occasionally I send things by Express Mail. I recently got an electronic "Smart Tag" to allow me to bypass the heaviest traffic in my city by using the Express Lane. I have even gotten my hair cut at Quick Cut. I really don't like waiting.

Wait Upon the Lord . . .

Isaiah 40:31 teaches us: "They that wait upon the LORD shall renew their strength; they shall mount up with wings as eagles; they shall run, and not be weary; and they shall walk, and not faint" (KJV). Almost every preacher I know has a good sermon based on this text. Most of us focus on the natural, almost homiletically obligatory three major points: mount up with wings as eagles, run and not grow weary, and walk and not faint.

But many of us neglect the "waiting upon the Lord" part.

On a recent bookstore visit, I saw a book with an intriguing title: *Don't Just Do Something, Sit There!* In our speeding world, that request falls on deaf ears. It is *hard* for a rapid-fire, super active, burn-candles-at-both-ends, pick-up-the-pace society to get to the place where just "sitting there" is acceptable.

Sue Monk Kidd told of an experience she had at a retreat at the St. Meinrad Archabbey. She had been fighting the need to keep in a perpetual motion mode for an extended period of time, and one day, with a heart full of "inner chaos," she saw a monk sitting very still beneath a tree. Impressed by his tranquility and focus, she paused to watch. Later that day she sought him out, confessed to him that she had great difficulty just doing nothing, and asked him how he could wait with such patience.

His response was, "Well, there's your problem right there, young lady. You've bought into the cultural myth that when you're waiting you're doing nothing." Then he added, "When you're waiting, you're *not* doing nothing. You're doing the most important something there is. You're allowing your soul to grow up. If you can't be still and wait, you can't become what God created you to be."

Have you ever heard Søren Kierkegaard's definition of sin? He wrote more than 100 years ago that "Sin is the steadfast refusal to be your one true self." Whatever hinders us from becoming the "person of God's creation" is to be rejected. Conversely, anything that aids us in the pursuit to discover who we really are will surely support our quest to know Whose we are.

Can our addiction to instantaneity be overcome? Sue Monk Kidd writes that she believes pursuing "quick and easy" can become addictive like other "process addictions." She declares that "we avoid our lives by moving faster and faster, going from one shortcut to another." She says growth is natural, but we use certain barriers repeatedly and compulsively that stop growth—this is our particular addiction.

What we need is *transformation*, rather than *renovation*. And transformation just doesn't happen impulsively or irresponsibly. It doesn't occur apart from deliberate effort and a resultant pain. And it requires waiting. It can't happen "cold turkey," or quickly. Transformation is not something that can be stumbled into, especially for those of us whose lives are characterized by the need to take action.

Len Sweet, the professor of evangelism at Drew University's Divinity School and a popular speaker and author, tells about his efforts to keep "starter" for sourdough bread alive. He, his friends, and his family have, in fact, been able to do that through the years by making sure that the "original" starter is refreshed and renewed as often as necessary. They have enjoyed many loaves of homemade bread because the initial batch of starter is "made new" each time the necessary ingredients are added. If that were not done, it would become useless and would have to be discarded.

Tools for Transformation

What are some practical ideas for reducing the speed of life? I will share a few ideas from several sources that have been helpful to me. Gordon Miller of World Vision International discussed several ideas for dealing with hurry sickness. These may be helpful in reversing the effects of living in a society addicted to haste. Here is part of his list, with my comments.

1. Change your attitude to life.

Another way of looking at this: if you can't change your life, try bending your attitude. Paul Tillich once wrote that reality is what we adjust to because it will not adjust to us. Very often it becomes crystal clear that "cooperating with the inevitable" is the only alternative available to us.

2. Cultivate a satisfying relationship with God.

Hurry sickness is at the base of many problems we have related to our intimacy with God. As we have seen, there are no hard and fast rules for one's personal faith formation. In fact, to imply that "rules" are the critical factor in one's spirituality may actually be counterproductive to such spiritual intimacy.

At the same time, I do believe that the one crucial component is having the time to focus on this important relationship, whether it is in the morning, the evening, or at several junctures during the day. I know someone who takes what he calls five-minute segments of time throughout every workday for the purpose of "recharging" his spiritual batteries.

3. Change your sleep habits so you get sufficient rest.
Sleep is like a lubricant for the body. When it is low, the friction between the body's systems wear down. Archibald Hart feels that the imposition of certain "rules" is necessary for good sleep. For example, even though the vast majority of people get less than seven hours of sleep per night, it is important to set a goal for a minimum of eight hours. Another goal is to get up and go to bed at the same time each day.

4. Develop supportive relationships.
The importance of a support system beyond the "normal" work and family relationships cannot be overestimated. My long-term participation in two ministry support groups was a highly significant experience for me. The first one, in Jacksonville, Alabama, was quite ecumenical and consisted of two Methodists, two Episcopalians, one Presbyterian, and one Baptist (me). It was the first time in my ministry that I had an in-depth relationship with anyone outside my own denominational tradition, and the

group quickly became an important part of my "family of faith" during my fourteen years there. That experience was so positive that I was elated to find another group when we moved to Clemson, South Carolina, in 1981. And this one became significant in many ways. We developed a strong bond, loved each other unconditionally, and lovingly challenged each other's poorly-thought-out assumptions. Any one of us would "go to the mat" for any of the others.

5. Use appropriate music to counter mood swings.
When I get to the office early, one of my most enjoyable activities to help my day get started is to put a CD into the player and just sit in my platform rocker. (I start my workday as soon as I get off my rocker.) I have come to enjoy the music of the masters, but J.S. Bach is my favorite. Although I don't fully understand why, no other composition moves me the way *Jesu, Joy of Man's Desiring* does, and I usually hear it at least once a day. Studies have revealed that listening to classical music slows down the heart rate and lowers blood pressure. My hunch is that such music also helps deal with hurry sickness.

6. Schedule daily exercise and relaxation.
Any need to justify this one? Our bodies need regular, fairly vigorous exercise to aid our quest toward health. And we need to be able to disengage from

the variety of stressors, which are a part of all our lives, and find a way to relax. Health and fitness centers can be a highly valuable tool in aiding the process of gaining health. But this is an area where good intentions are not enough. Fitness is not achieved by carrying around the membership card. For it to be of any help, you have to use it.

7. Slowing.

In the U.S. there is a developing phenomenon known as "slowing." Essentially, slowing is about a movement to slow down, concentrating on the tension that exists between "slower/better" vs. "faster/cheaper." Some components of the movement focus on the basics of life—food, work, nature—while others challenge an ideology of a society that is apparently bent on widening the gap between the "haves" and the "have-nots."

How realistic is it to consciously and deliberately slow the pace of our lives? It isn't easy for most of us who have become addicted to haste.

One morning toward the end of this writing project, I had a conversation with my wife before I left for work. It was during the summer when she, as a teacher, had the luxury of sleeping later if she wished. I had gotten up early and had already gone for my walk. I had already had a leisurely breakfast and was reading the morning paper when she came in the room. She asked if I was going to work since it was approaching the time for our building to open. That's when I told her about "slowing." I said that I was practicing this new thing and taking my time rather than rushing to the office. She looked at me with that "yeah, right!" look and after a chortle or two, wondered if I was going to practice that on the other end of the day.

I told her that I had made a mid-year resolution—after all the research I had done on hurry sickness, I am going to practice slowing the pace of my life. In fact, I had already been practicing by intentionally getting in the slower driving lanes on the commute to and from the office; also, I had already practiced choosing the longer check-out lines at the grocery store and even letting others ahead of me. She already knew that I had slowed the pace of eating meals.

Further, I related to her that I had begun to become more deliberate in establishing boundaries and creating the margins necessary to avoid short-circuiting plans. And I think the one thing I said to her about which she was the most cynical was, "I am saying 'no' to some requests on my time."

I also confessed to her how hard it had been. It is not easy for me to get out of the habit of trying to sneak eleven items through the express lane at the grocery store or leaving early for an appointment so that I can avoid the strain of getting there just in the nick of time. And the most difficult lesson I am learning is that after about 40 years of feeling that I must be pretty important to have been asked to do this special task, I need to practice saying "no." My sense of worth really is not determined by the number of commitments on my calendar, the number of activities I am involved in, or the number of hours per day I work. Such worth comes from the creative work of God.

Moving in Normal Time

A friend told me a story about what happened one Sunday morning as he was driving on Interstate 64 to a preaching engagement. He looked to his left and saw a woman in a brand new Honda CRV doing 70 miles per hour while looking in her rear-view mirror and putting on eyeliner. He looked away for a couple of seconds, and when he looked back she was halfway over in his lane, still working on her makeup! He swerved a bit to the right and honked his horn.

He was so annoyed at her dangerous multitasking that he dropped his electric shaver, which knocked the donut out of his other hand. While trying to straighten out the car using his knees against the steering wheel, his cell phone fell away from his ear and it (the phone, not the ear) fell into the cup of coffee between his legs, splashing it out and burning his legs. The worst thing about it all, he said, was that his phone was ruined and he was disconnected from an important call—all because of that other driver!

Well . . . that story is *slightly* embellished, but it does point out some of the problems that hurry can produce in our busy lives. Recently, I was standing in the lobby of a building waiting for the elevator to take me to the 12th floor. I had already pressed the "up" button and it was clearly illuminated. Before the elevator arrived, several others had joined me and at least three of them pushed the button, one of them multiple times (presumably he thought the button was hooked to an accelerator of some sort that would put the elevator in the *express* mode). Then, when it finally came and we entered, the same guy pushed the "close door" button four or five times!

We have explored why so many of us seem to be constantly in a rush and that haste has become a pervasive societal disease, even an addiction. One of the great ironies of our time is that we rush in order to have more leisure time. Perhaps the parking lot at any American mall is one of the best metaphors we could find to describe this frenetic malaise. The goal is always to get as close as possible to the store you want to visit. Parking becomes an exercise of wit, driving skill, and physics. Dirty looks and obscene gestures are the order of the day as shoppers angle for the best parking advantage they can get. We go through all of this fuss and frustration because we want to save a little extra time—but instead we find the pace of our entire lives has increased. We *never* get to feel we have extra time!

"The Hurrier I Go, the Behinder I Get"

How many times during the course of a typical day have you either heard or made comments about time? "Can you believe that summer is almost over? It has been like a *blur* to me." "Christmas will be here before you know it!" I had a high school basketball coach who started every practice with, "We have a long way to go and a short time to get there . . . so let's hurry and get a move on!"

We are the modern equivalent of Pavlov's dogs, suggests Dr. Ann McGee-Cooper. Our current "bells" are the timepieces by which we order our lives—watches, alarm clocks, calendars, and the like. They are the external controls that govern how our internal lives are run. The often-subliminal message of the clock that is ground into our consciousness is that we need to hurry because time is getting away from us.

One of the most bizarre stories I have ever heard was from a Reader's Digest account I read in my dentist's office. Taking a cue from the fast-food industry, a funeral home director proposed to construct a drive-through viewing window for people who just don't have the time to come inside. The director is reported to have said that people these days are just too busy with their work and other things: "This is just one way to make it easier for them to view the deceased, sign the book to show that you dropped by, and get on with the day."

Stop and Smell the Roses

Stacy Hawkins Adams, a columnist with the *Richmond Times-Dispatch*, told in her July 27, 2002, column of an experience she had in the grocery store. She said if the store had traffic cops, she would have received a speeding ticket. Her husband was preparing his first sermon at their church, and her plans included the culinary delights appropriate for the occasion. To complicate things, members of her husband's family were coming to visit and the meal would be much larger than usual, and she had to ride herd on a couple of preschoolers. Her schedule was busy and she buzzed through the store's aisles "like Speedy Gonzales on a sugar high." Her goal was to shop for groceries in record time in order to save time for other items on her agenda.

She raced through the store as if she were competing in a 100-meter sprint. That's when it happened. At the end of one aisle, she turned the corner so quickly that she almost smashed into another woman's cart. Stacy apologized as the other shopper smiled and pulled her cart aside to let her pass. With no hint of anger or anxiety, the woman simply said, "I can tell you're in a hurry."

Stacy signaled "thank you" with a measure of humility and resumed shopping. But as she continued to shop, she slowed her pace. By the time she saw the woman again, she was downright casual. She commented to the woman, "I've slowed down." The woman chuckled and then gently added what Stacy called a gem: "It's okay to take our time. Time moves too fast, anyway. Whenever we can, we should savor it. Remember that when you're tempted to rush."

Right there in the cereal aisle, Stacy realized she had received a valuable piece of wisdom, something to remind her of what was really important. She had fallen into the hurry trap, but here was an older woman reminding her that even with a frenzied schedule, she had the capacity to move in "normal time"—and in the process, fully value the present.

Stacy's encounter in the grocery store with a woman who apparently had learned the secret of "slowing" made a profound impression on her. For the rest of that day, she found herself taking time to read to her daughter, play with her son, talk to a neighbor, and catch up with an old friend by telephone. Further, she handled interruptions with patience and grace. And a couple of days later, when the family finally got to enjoy the results of her time and effort, "I remembered just how long those cakes had been in the making. I savored each bite."

The apostle Paul wrote some very practical advice to the members of the church at Ephesus: "Be very careful, then, how you live—not as unwise but as wise, making the most of every opportunity, because the days are evil" (Ephesians 5:15–16). The phrase "making the most of every opportunity" is language borrowed from the marketplace. A Scripture that is taken seriously by all shoppers worthy of their name, it literally means, "snapping up all the bargains that are available." Paul is thinking about the use of God's gift of time and he calls those who snap up all of God's bargains "wise."

Jesus and His Psalm Pilot

Can you imagine Jesus focusing His life and ministry around a small handheld computer? "Let's see now . . . today I have a 2:00 o'clock staff meeting with the disciples—we must go over some training on the casting out of demons. Then, at noon I need to meet that woman at the well. Next Tuesday I have a meeting with James and John about that promotion they are asking about and dinner plans with Mary, Martha, and Lazarus. I could fit a healing in at 10:00 that day. Will that work for you?"

Sounds pretty ridiculous, doesn't it? As we have said, Jesus was never in a hurry. And there has never been a more balanced life than His. Jesus seemed to operate by a "Psalm Pilot" rather than a PalmPilot. Remember, reformer Martin Luther was said to have been a very busy man with all the administrative work, preaching, teaching, and helping the students at the university. And he confessed that he would never have had the time to accomplish it all if he did not pray the psalms for three hours every day!

The Book of Psalms is a great place to begin and end. For example, Psalm 62:1 says, "For God alone my soul waits in silence; from him comes my salvation" (NRSV). The importance of a quiet, receptive heart can never be overstated. But it is so hard to do, much harder than it sounds. When we try to sit quietly in our noisy culture, we begin to notice how dependent we are on noise—television, conversation, music—often to distract us from what's really going on inside.

We may discover that we turn to these things to numb our pain or loneliness and that this constant static in our lives keeps us from recognizing the true state of our parched souls. As Dallas Willard has written, "Silence is frightening because it strips us as nothing else does, throwing us upon the stark realities of our life." It is scary sometimes to have our souls laid bare before God. And that's what often happens.

One of the most central and ancient practices of Christian prayer is called *Lectio Divina,* divine reading. It is a form of meditation—a slow, prayerful reading of the Scriptures or a passage of inspired writing. By reading the text slowly several times, word by word, and listening carefully for God's voice, you enter into and are surrounded by the text. Traditionally, one person would read a Bible passage aloud. Silence would follow. The text would be read again, and again. After the listeners had heard the text, they would leave and spend time in prayer and silence.

For a culture that is chronically sleep-deprived, stressed, and anxious, working more hours than ever before, hooked on cell phones, pagers, email, and other gadgets designed to give us more time, the word we desperately need to hear is that there is a better way. It is *not* God's plan for us to rush through life barely skimming its surface.

Hear (*shema* and *akouein*) the familiar word from Romans 12 with new ears, through Eugene Peterson's *The Message*:

> "So here's what I want you to do, God helping you: Take your everyday, ordinary life—your sleeping, eating, going-to-work, and walking-around life—and place it before God as an offering. Embracing what God does for you is the best thing you can do for him. Don't

become so well-adjusted to your culture that you fit into it without even thinking. Instead, fix your attention on God. You'll be changed from the inside out. Readily recognize what he wants from you, and quickly respond to it. Unlike the culture around you, always dragging you down to its level of immaturity, God brings the best out of you, develops well-formed maturity in you."

—Romans 12:1–2

Scriptures for Treating Hurry Sickness

"By the seventh day God had finished the work he had been doing; so on the seventh day he rested from all his work. And God blessed the seventh day and made it holy, because on it he rested from all the work of creating that he had done."

—Genesis 2:2–3

"Six days do your work, but on the seventh day do not work, so that your ox and your donkey may rest and the slave born in your household, and the alien as well, may be refreshed."

—Exodus 23:12

"The LORD replied, 'My Presence will go with you, and I will give you rest.'"

—Exodus 33:14

"The LORD is my shepherd, I shall not be in want. He makes me lie down in green pastures, he leads me beside quiet waters, he restores my soul. He guides me in paths of righteousness for his name's sake."

—Psalm 23:1–3

"*Be still before the* L*ord* *and wait patiently for him.*"

—Psalm 37:7*a*

"*This is the day the* L*ord* *has made; let us rejoice and be glad in it.*"

—Psalm 118:24

"*My heart is not proud, O* L*ord,*
    my eyes are not haughty;
I do not concern myself with great matters
    or things too wonderful for me.
But I have stilled and quieted my soul;
    like a weaned child with its mother,
    like a weaned child is my soul within me.
O Israel, put your hope in the L*ord*
    both now and forevermore."

—Psalm 131

"*You will keep in perfect peace him whose mind is steadfast, because he trusts in you.*"

—Isaiah 26:3

"*This is what the Sovereign* L*ord, the Holy One of Israel, says: 'In repentance and rest is your salvation, in quietness and trust is your strength, but you would have none of it.'*"

—Isaiah 30:15

"The fruit of righteousness will be peace; the effect of righteousness will be quietness and confidence forever. My people will live in peaceful dwelling places, in secure homes, in undisturbed places of rest."
                                        —Isaiah 32:17–18

"Do you not know? Have you not heard? The LORD is the everlasting God, the Creator of the ends of the earth. He will not grow tired or weary, and his understanding no one can fathom. He gives strength to the weary and increases the power of the weak. Even youths grow tired and weary, and young men stumble and fall; but those who hope in the LORD will renew their strength. They will soar on wings like eagles; they will run and not grow weary, they will walk and not be faint."
                                        —Isaiah 40:28–31

"It is good to wait quietly for the salvation of the LORD."
                                        —Lamentations 3:26

"Therefore I tell you, do not worry about your life, what you will eat or drink; or about your body, what you will wear. Is not life more important than food, and the body more important than clothes? Look at the birds of the air; they do not sow or reap or store away in barns, and yet your heavenly Father feeds them. Are you not much more valuable than they? Who of you by worrying can add a single hour to his life?"
                                        —Matthew 6:25–27

"Come to me, all you who are weary and burdened, and I will give you rest. Take my yoke upon you and learn from me, for I am gentle and humble in heart, and you will find rest for your souls. For my yoke is easy and my burden is light."

—Matthew 11:28–30

"Then, because so many people were coming and going that they did not even have a chance to eat, he said to them, 'Come with me by yourselves to a quiet place and get some rest.' So they went away by themselves in a boat to a solitary place."

—Mark 6:31–32

"But if we hope for what we do not yet have, we wait for it patiently."

—Romans 8:25

"Be patient, then, brothers, until the Lord's coming. See how the farmer waits for the land to yield its valuable crop and how patient he is for the autumn and spring rains. You too, be patient and stand firm, because the Lord's coming is near."

—James 5:7–8